William Henry Long

A Dictionary of the Isle of Wight Dialect, and of Provincialisms used in the Island

William Henry Long

A Dictionary of the Isle of Wight Dialect, and of Provincialisms used in the Island

ISBN/EAN: 9783337153076

Printed in Europe, USA, Canada, Australia, Japan

Cover: Foto ©ninafisch / pixelio.de

More available books at **www.hansebooks.com**

A DICTIONARY

OF THE

ISLE OF WIGHT DIALECT,

And of Provincialisms used in the Island;

WITH ILLUSTRATIVE ANECDOTES AND TALES;

TO WHICH IS APPENDED

THE CHRISTMAS BOYS' PLAY,

AN ISLE OF WIGHT "HOOAM HARVEST,"

AND

SONGS SUNG BY THE PEASANTRY;

FORMING

A Treasury of Insular Manners and Customs

OF FIFTY YEARS AGO.

BY W. H. LONG.

(Subscribers' Edition.)

LONDON:
REEVES & TURNER, 196 STRAND, W.C.
ISLE OF WIGHT:
G. A. BRANNON & CO., "COUNTY PRESS,"
ST. JAMES'S SQUARE, NEWPORT.
1886.

LIST OF SUBSCRIBERS.

Mrs. Aston, Bargate Street, Southampton.
J. R. Blake, Esq., Stone House, Blackwater, I.W.
A. Brannon, Esq., Gatcombe Newbarn, I.W.
Lieut.-Gen. The Hon. Somerset J. G. Calthorpe, J.P., Woodlands Vale, Ryde, I.W.
J. L. Cantelo, Esq., River Avon Street, Liverpool.
J. F. Childs, Esq., Southsea.
C. Conquest, Esq., 66 Denbigh Street, London.
J. Cooke, Esq., Langton House, Gosport.
The Rev. Sir W. H. Cope, Bart., Bramshill, Hants.
Colonel Crozier, West Hill, Yarmouth, I.W.
Colonel L. D. H. Currie, Ventnor, I.W.
Dr. G. H. R. Dabbs, Highfields, Shanklin, I.W.
A. Harbottle Estcourt, Esq., Deputy Governor of the Isle of Wight, Standen Elms, I.W.
Sidney Everett, Esq., Fairmount, Shanklin, I.W.
A. T. Everitt, Esq., Portsmouth.
W. Featon Fisher, Esq., St. Bartholomew's Hospital, London.
J. Lewis Ffytche, Esq., F.S.A., Freshwater, I.W.
Mrs. Fleming, Roude, I.W.
T. Francis, Esq., Havant.
Messrs. W. George's Sons, Bristol.
J. Griffin, Esq., J.P., Southsea.
Dr. J. Groves, Carisbrooke, I.W.
A. Howell, Esq., Carnarvon, Southsea.
T. Howell, Esq., St. David's, Southsea.

List of Subscribers.

The Rev. E. B. James, Carisbrooke Vicarage, I.W.
T. D. A. Jewers, Esq., Free Library, Portsmouth.
G. F. Jones, Esq., Afton Manor, Freshwater, I.W.
F. E. Knott, Esq., M.R.C.V.S., Portsmouth.
O. Lasbury, Esq., Cotham, Bristol.
George Long, Esq., Newport, I.W.
The Rev. H. J. Maddock, Tremadoc, Shanklin, I.W.
W. B. Mew, Esq., The Polars, Newport, I.W.
Qr.-Mr.-Sergt. H. Morey, 2nd Batt. Royal Irish Rifles, Halifax, Nova Scotia.
C. E. Mumby, Esq., Gosport.
F. Murray, Esq., Derby.
J. Nield, Esq., Bath Street, Bristol.
E. Parsons, Esq., Brompton, London.
W. Payne, Esq., Woodleigh, Southsea.
R. Roach Pittis, Esq., Marl Hill, Carisbrooke, I.W.
G. W. Pragnell, Esq., Claridge's Hotel, London.
W. H. Riddett, Esq., Ryde, I.W.
S. J. A. Salter, Esq., F.R.S., Basingfield, Basingstoke.
Thomas Self, Esq., Newport, I.W.
John Spickernell, Esq., Field House, Carisbrooke, I.W.
Fred'c. Stratton, Esq., The Chantry House, Newport, I.W.
W. T. Stratton, Esq., Bury Hill, Carisbrooke, I.W.
The Rev. E. Summers, Brading Vicarage, I.W.
The Honourable Hallam Tennyson, Farringford House, Freshwater, I.W.
Miss Urry, Gatcombe Hill, I.W.
F. W. B. Waterworth, Esq., Newport, I.W.
Edward Watts, Esq., Thetis House, West Cowes, I.W.
W. Self Weeks, Esq., F.R.H.S., Clitheroe.
F. White-Popham, Esq., Deputy Lieutenant of the Isle of Wight, Wootton Lodge, Wootton, I.W.

PREFACE.

The following pages aim at giving—besides a Dictionary of the dialect—illustrations of the use of the words, and specimens of the every-day talk and forms of expression current among the peasantry of the Isle of Wight. The list of words could easily have been made more extensive, but many found in other parts of the country as well as in the Island have been purposely omitted; although a number equally as common have been retained, from a desire to make the collection as complete a transcript as possible of the provincial vernacular. The Glossary of Isle of Wight Words edited by Mr. C. R. Smith for the English Dialect Society has been of the greatest service in the compilation of this, (though the larger part of the matter here printed was collected before its appearance in 1881); and considerable assistance has been afforded by the Glossary of Hampshire Words compiled by the Rev. Sir W. H. Cope for the same Society. Akerman's Glossary of Wiltshire Words and Barnes' Glossary of the Dorset Dialect have also been occasionally consulted.

No one knows better than the compiler that a Dictionary like the present must necessarily be more or less incomplete; but he hopes that not many words of importance will be found to have been omitted; and such as it is—he offers the result of his labour to the favourable consideration of his fellow-Islanders, and the Public generally.

W. H. L.

CONTENTS.

	PAGE
INTRODUCTION	ix.
DICTIONARY OF THE ISLE OF WIGHT DIALECT	1
PLAY ACTED BY THE "CHRISTMAS BOYS" . .	99
AN ISLAND "HOOAM HARVEST" . . .	109
SONGS SUNG BY THE PEASANTRY . . .	125
SUPPLEMENTARY LIST OF WORDS	168

INTRODUCTION.

The provincial dialects spoken in the southern counties of England, once forming part of the Saxon Kingdom of Wessex, have many general features of resemblance, showing that they all are branches from one parent stock. Many of the provincialisms current in the Isle of Wight are the same as, or very similar to, those found in the adjoining counties of Hampshire, Wilts, and Dorset; but a good proportion seems to be peculiar to the Island; and the dialect of Sussex on the one side, and of Somerset and Devon on the other, are very different from the insular vernacular. The basis of the dialect of the Isle of Wight is purely Anglo-Saxon, and it is remarkable, considering its situation, and intercourse (principally through fishing and smuggling) with the opposite coast of France, that scarcely a word of undoubted French origin seems to have been introduced.

The ever-increasing number of visitors flocking into the Island, and the growing influences of Board Schools, are rapidly sweeping away all vestiges of the native Island speech, while the older inhabitants abstain as much as possible from using it in the presence of strangers; and the rising generation are growing up ignorant of the meaning of words still used by their grandfathers,—some of them far more expressive and comprehensive than their modern substitutes. For instance,—what a combination of common every-day phrases is necessary to explain the influence of dry weather on ripened corn, expressed by an Island labourer in two words—" bret out"; or to give the full meaning he comprises in the single word "snoodle." There is no doubt that by the gradual disappearance of the local dialects, various words and forms of expression are lost, which modern English replaces but imperfectly.

Many of the peculiarities of transposition of letters, and of pronunciation, will be found noted in their places in the

Dictionary, but there are a few forms which may be noted more at length. The vowels and consonants are always transposed in such words as—

hapse	for	*hasp*
clapse	,,	*clasp*
wopse	,,	*wasp*, &c.

The diphthong *oi* is pronounced *wi*, e.g.—

spwile	for	*spoil*
bwoy	,,	*boy*
bwile or *bwyle*	,,	*boil*
pwison	,,	*poison*

The old English affix, *en*, is often added to adjectives, as— *timberen* (made of wood, or wooden), *earthen, leatheren, elmen* —or more commonly, *ellem*,—*ashen* (made of elm or ash); and in verbs ending in *en*, the last syllable is generally dropped, as—"Sharp my riphook," for "Sharpen my reaping hook"; "I sholl fat my pig," for "I shall fatten my pig"; and so on. The past tense of many irregular, as well as regular verbs, is generally formed by adding *ed* to the present tense, as—

Present.	*Past.*		
bear	beared	*instead of*	bore
blow	blowed	,,	blew
drink	drinked	,,	drank
feel	feeled	,,	felt
grow	growed	,,	grew
hold	holded	,,	held
know	knowed	,,	knew
lead	leaded	,,	led
lend	lended	,,	lent
sting	stinged	,,	stung
spend	spended	,,	spent

and many others.

The conjugation of the verb "To be," in the Island, is as follows:—

INDICATIVE MOOD.—*Present Tense.*

		Interrogatively.	
Sing.	*Plural.*	*Sing.*	*Plural.*
I be	We be	Be I?	Be we?
Thee bist	You be	Bist?	Be you?
He *or* she is	They be	Ezza?	Be um?

Introduction.

Past Tense.

I was	We was
Thee wast	You was
He was	They was

Future.   Interrogatively.

I sholl *or* wull	We sholl *or* wull	Wull I?	Wull we?
Thee shat *or* wull	You sholl *or* wull	Wut thee?	Wull 'ee?
He sholl *or* wull	They sholl *or* wull	Wull he?	Wull um?

POTENTIAL MOOD.—Past Tense.

I med a ben	We med a ben
Thee medst a ben	You med a ben
He med a ben	They med a ben

IMPERATIVE.

Thee'st better be	We better be
Let'n be	
Mak'n be	Make um be

Thee is generally used for *thy*, as—" Hast had thee nammet it, mayet?" But in such a phrase as " Hast *thee* had thee nammet, mayet?" the first *thee* is strongly emphasized.

The objective cases of the personal pronouns *he, she,* and *it* are pronounced *en*, or more correctly, *'n; them* being *um. She* is generally represented by *her*, and conversely.

Can't her git'n down?	Can't she get him down?
I don't want noo truck wi' she.	I wish to have nothing to do with her.
Let'n bide, wull'ee!	Let him alone, will you!
I louz he'll gee'n to'n.	I think he will give it to him.
Drow um down 'bout house.	Throw them down on the floor.
Let goo on 'en, casn't!	Let it [*or* him] go, can't you!

The nominative of the pronouns is also generally used instead of the inflected cases, as—

What use wull he be to *we*?	What use will he [*or* it] be to us?
He never opened his mouth to *we* about it.	
I sholl talk to *he* about that.	
I never met wi' *she* all the time I was there.	

The possessive pronouns *hers, ours, yours, theirs*, terminate in *n*.

That yeppern es *hern*, edden't it? That apron is hers, isn't it?
That 'ere pig's *ourn*.
Edden't this 'ere hoe *yourn?*
Don't ye titch they apples,—they be *theirn*.

As a contrast, and to show the progress of refinement in the Island dialect, a document is here given, written in 1790 by a parish clerk or overseer; and an epistle addressed to the master of a Board school, by a mother, in 1880.

"Whit Munday 1790.

"A mayn of cocks to fite for three ginneys prise, the sekunt best cock to have a hat for a faver, and 8 cocks only; and nayther cock to be over four pouns and a haf, to fite in the parish of Northwood, and to meet by 10 a clock, and to way by 11, and hosoever is a mind to putt in a cock must give in there names to John Dore, and to putt down haf a crown, and hosoever is not there to time, to forfit there haf a crown."

Thus much for 1790; now for a specimen of 1880, the writer of which is evidently of the opinion that education should be paid for by the piece, or by contract.

"Mister N—— If you pleas my Johnny went to school this morning and I sent three apence and I told him that he was to tell you that he would bring tother apeny after he come home to dinner and you send him back again for three apence more and he did not come to school only a day and a haf last week and he brought a peny and I am sure that is enuff for a day and a haf and he havent been michen for I kept him at home to help me and you send him home again three times for a nother peny and if Mister P—— comes to me I shall tell he the rayson of it all he shall bring another peny when he goes to school in the morning and if you sends him back anymore I shall keep him away altogether and send him somewhere else.—Yours, &c."

Another epistolary specimen, almost pathetic in its simplicity, is as follows :—

"Orgest the seventeen 100880. Mr. N—— Will you plese to let my darter lissey have half a day to come home in the afternoon because her granmother is very near dead for she got something the matter with her to legs and I got to go to Mister B——s sowing at three a clock and she as nobody to mind the house nor give her her medcen and oblige yours truely ——."

In conclusion, a reply received by a lady in answer to her advertisement for a general servant is appended. It is *verbatim et literatim.*

"dear friend I heard that you was in wont of a searvent wich Miss —— reckamened me to you I ware gannril searvent at Mrs —— 3 years and 3 mainths I had 8 pounds a year and my washing put out I want 11 pounds a yeer I am 320 years old in Janivary you repli at Mrs —— for my charocter."

DICTIONARY

OF THE

ISLE OF WIGHT DIALECT.

A.

A is pronounced broad and long, and is generally used instead of the pronoun "he."

"A zed a should hay zum on't by next Zadderday."—He said he should have some of it by next Saturday.

AATER. After. Aaternoon—afternoon.

AATERCLAPS. Something disagreeable happening in a matter which is considered settled.

"I don't want noo aaterclaps."—I don't want anything after this: let the matter be ended.

AILS. Beards of barley; as Barley ails.

ACT. To behave or speak in an affected manner, to play tricks.

"Dedn't he jest about act, and make hisself zote!"—Didn't he behave in an affected manner, and make himself look silly!

ADONE. A command to stop or cease.

"Adone, I tell 'ee."—Cease, I tell you.

AFEARED. Afraid, frightened.

"I be afeared to go annearst un."—I am afraid to go near it.

"Be not *affeared*, the Isle is full of noises."
—*Tempest.* iii. 2.

AGEN. Against.

"He vell agen it."—He fell against it. "To run up agen" anything or person.—To meet with it casually or by chance. "I sholl run up agen 'en one of these days."—I shall meet with him at some time or other.

AGONE, or AGOO. Ago, since.
"'Tes dree year agoo now this zummer zunce we lived at Rue Street."—It is three years ago now this summer since we lived at Rue Street.

ALL OF A HOOGH (the *hoogh* guttural). Out of shape, or place; all on one side.
"That ere wut rick is all of a hoogh."—That oat rick is out of shape, or all on one side.

ALLZIDES. All together, every one.
"We be gwyne to begin dreshen allzides to-morrow mornen." We are all going to begin threshing to morrow morning.

ANNEARST. Near.
"Don't goo annearst the mare, she med fling at ye."—Don't go near the mare, she might kick you.

ANEWSE. Very like; much, or very nearly the same thing.
"I was down at varmer Vlux's yesterday, you, and zid that gurt Sall Jooans there. She *do* goo on, I can tell 'ee, jest as if she was missus. D'ye think the wold man's married to her?"
"I dunno, but I louz 'tes anewse the saame, you."

ANJUR DOGS. Andirons, at the sides of a hearth to support the logs, and with hooks for the spit to run on.

APPLESTUCKLEN. A small apple pie or tart, baked without a dish.

ARENEST. A small sum of money paid down to bind a bargain.
"I paad 'en ten shillens in arenest vor the pigs."—I paid him ten shillings to bind the bargain for the pigs.

ASH. A stubble field, after the corn has been cut and carted.
"Bwoy, drave the cows out into the wheat ash."—Boy, drive the cows into the wheat ash.

ASPRAWL. Sprawling.
"A was zo drunk, a vell out o' the chair all asprawl bout house."—He was so drunk, he fell out of the chair sprawling on the floor.

ASTROUT. Stretched out stiffly, as frozen linen.
"My vingers be all astrout wi' the coold."—My fingers are stiff with cold.

ATHERT. Across, athwart.
"Be you gwyne athert to-day?"—Are you going across [the water to Portsmouth or Southampton] to-day? "The hare run right athert the ground."—The hare ran straight across the field.

Isle of Wight Dialect.

Auverdrow. To overthrow, to upset.

"He auverdrode the waggon gwyne down the shoot."—He upset the waggon going down the hill.

Auver-right. Opposite.

"A used to live auver-right wold Chessel's, out at Banger's Whistle."—He used to live opposite old Chessel's, at Banger's Whistle.

Avore. Before.

"I sholl be there avore you."—I shall be there before you.

Avoord. To afford.

Ax. To ask or inquire, to publish the banns of marriage.

"He axed me to litter-up vor'n."—He asked me to put the straw bedding under the horses for him. "I zay you; Bob Gubbins and Poll Trot was *axed* in Atherton Church last Zunday."

Azew. Dry, not giving milk.

"The cows be all azew."—The cows give no milk. "I went up to varmer Baker's to zee if I could git a drap o' milk to make a traykel posset wi', for the wold dooman's coold. 'Noa,' a said, 'I wants moor milk than I got vor the pigs, ver near all the cows be gone azew.'"

B.

Baaks. Spots in an arable field not properly ploughed.

Backside. A farmyard behind, or close to, the house.

"Playse Mister Newman, father toold me to come up and ax you if you'd lett'n putt hes keert into your backside till to-morrow mornen."

Back up. To support anyone by money or influence.

Bacon rack. A frame hanging from the ceiling of the kitchen of a farm house, on which smoked hams and bacon are kept.

Badger. To tease, to importune anyone.

Bad off. To be poor, in a state of poverty.

"They be miserable bad off: I louz 'tes terbul hard does wi' 'em."—They are very poor: I imagine it is very bad times with them.

Bailey. A farm bailiff, a sheriff's officer.

BALLYRAG. To abuse or vituperate, to use scurrilous language.

"Dedn't the wold dooman gimme a ballyraggen!"—Didn't the old woman abuse or scold me!

BANNICK. To beat, or knock about.

BARGAN. A small farm or property; often a house and garden.

"He got a small bargan in Niton parish."

BARGAN ZADDERDAY. There were three of these,—"Vust, Middle, and last Bargan Zadderday,"—being the three Saturdays immediately before Old Michaelmas Day, Oct. 11th; and they were the fixed times for hiring yearly farm servants. Fifty years ago, hundreds of male and female farm servants, in their best attire, flocked into Newport on these Saturdays from all parts of the Island: it was their annual fête days; the women assembling at "Gape Mouth Corner," opposite the Vine Inn, and the men taking their station in the "Beast Market" After hiring themselves, and settling the locality of their next year's service, with hats bedecked with ribbons they crowded the dancing rooms of certain well known and popular inns, as the "Red Lion," the "Lamb," and above all, "Bell Cham'-ber," where soon the fun and dissipation became fast and furious; quarrels arose; and rivals, to settle "who was best man," adjourned to "Trattle's Butt" to fight it out; and a scene of riot and boisterous revelling generally concluded each "Bargan Zadderday."

BARROW PIG. A young boar castrated.

BATTER. To dig or scrape furiously, with small effect; the action of a fowl in cleaning itself.

BATTS. Short ridges, odd corners in ploughed fields.

BATTLEDORE. A child's first primer, containing the alphabet, numerals, &c., on thick coarse paper, made to fold; generally sold by pedlars.

"You shall not neede to buy bookes, no, scorne to distinguish a B from a Battledore."—*Gul's Horne-booke*, 1609.

BAY. An obstruction in the course of a ditch or small stream, so as to form a pool.

BEAT UP. State of being, or health.

"How d'ye sim to beät up, mayet?"—How do you do? or, How are you getting on?

BECALL. To abuse, to call bad names.

"He becalled me everything he could think on."

BEEAST. Oxen, cattle.

"Bist thee gwyne to sar the becast, Jack?"—Are you going to feed the cattle, Jack?

BEE BUTT. A beehive.

BELT. To beat or thrash.

"I'll gi' ye a middlen belten predney."—I'll give you a severe beating presently.

BELVE. To bellow as a bull, to roar when beaten.

BEN. Been; also, a bin for corn.

"Take the ziv off the wut ben, wull'ee you, and drow'n into the hull coop."—Take the sieve off the oat bin, will you, and throw it into the "hull coop" [*which see*].

BETHWINE. Wild clematis, or convolvulus.

BEVAST. To put the dripping on meat roasting; also, to beat.

"I'll gi' thee a good beyasten as soon as we be out end."—I'll give you a good beating as soon as we get to the end of the furrow, or field.

BIDE *(Ang.-Sax. bidan).* To abide, stay, or dwell.

"He bides zumwhere about Keasbrooke."—He stays somewhere in Carisbrooke.

BILLHOOK. A short-handled curved wood chopper, used by hedgers, and for domestic use.

BILLUS. The bellows; also, to pant after hard running.

"Comin up that shoot ded gimme a billusen, I can tell 'ee."—Coming up that hill quite winded me, I can tell you.

BILLY BITER. The blue titmouse.

BINDER. A large quantity (generally of food).

"We had liver and crow vor dinner, and I ded take in a binder—I shan't want noo moor grub to-day."—We had pig's liver for dinner, and I ate such a lot that I shall want no more food to-day.

BITTEL. A wooden maul or very large mallet, used in cleaving wood or "tying out" horses; when used in driving stakes in making a hedge, called a "stakebittel."

"I left my stakebittel out in the ground last week, and the zun's ben and warped 'en all to pieces."—I left my stakebittel out in the field last week, and the sun has split it all to pieces.

BIVVER *(A.S. bifian)*. To flicker, to quiver; also to tremble or shake.

"I could see the lightnen bivveren about in the element."— I could see the lightning flickering or flashing in the sky. "I sims all of a bivver wi' the cooald."—I tremble or shake with the cold.

BLACKTHORN WINTER. A second or short winter, a week or two of cold weather occurring in the early spring.

BLARE. To bellow, to low as a cow, to cry.

"The wold dooman went sniffen and blaren about the plaace, like a wold cow that's lost her calf."

BLEYADS. The shafts of a cart or waggon.

BLOODSTICK. A small and short, but thick, wooden stick, used to strike the lancet (fleyams) when bleeding cattle.

BLOW OUT. A good feed, a very full meal.

"Dedn't they there teetotallers hay a blow out yesterday; I heerd my wold dooman zay she drinked zixteen cups o' tay."

BODY HOSS. The horse in the team nearest the "thiller," or horse in the shafts.

BOME. To swagger in walking, to swing about.

"He bomed into church as if he was Lord Holmes."

BOMESWISH. To ride or drive fast.

"I met wold varmer Taalor and hes missus in their new pony keert, gwyne bomeswish over Staplers."

BONNYGOO. Lively or spirited.

"That's a bonnygoo hoss o' yourn, varmer."—Thats a spirited horse you have, farmer.

BOOR STAG. An old boar, castrated.

"Last week wold buttcher Smith come up to our plaace, and a zed, 'Hav'ee got ar a calf to zill?' 'Iss,' I zays, 'I have, but he's onny dree days wold.' 'Never mind that,' a zed; zoo he bought'n. 'Well,' I zays, 'I spooase you'll putt'n to another cow, won't ye?' 'Noa I shan't,' a zed, 'I sholl kill'n. I be gwyne to kill a wold boor stag, and I sholl make 'em booath into sassages; pork and veal, ye know, makes the best o' sassages.' 'Lar a massy!' I zays, 'I'll never yet noo moore sassages as long as I be alive; noo veal dree days wold, nor noo tough wold boor stag, vor me.'"

BOTHER. A difficulty, a disturbance.

BOTTOM. The valley or hollow between two downs.

"There's a good many rabbits, you, about Vairney Bottom, t'other side o' Gallibury Bump."—"Vairney" or Ferny Bottom is a remarkable depression in a "bottom" of the downs between Calbourne and Shorwell; and "Gallibury Bump" is an ancient tumulus on the top of Newbarn Down.

BOUT HOUSE. On the floor, or on the ground.

"Don't dro the things bout house."—Don't throw the things on the floor. "I was gwyne along out handy Lake one time, and I met wi' wold Juniper, as we used to call'n, crucklen along the zide o' the road. 'Hollo, Juniper!' I zays, 'thee doesn't look as if thee couldst auver dro a mill pond to-day;' and I'd noo zooner spoke than he up vist, and I vound myzelf bout house."

BOWLDISH. A wooden bowl with a handle.

"There goes Will Morris, wi' his hear cut round as if he'd putt the bowldish on his head."

BRAKE. A rough uncultivated piece of ground.

BRASH. Rash, impetuous.

"Dont'ee be too brash wi' that staff hook."

BREED. To plait.

"I was in the steyabul, zet down on the wut ben, breeden the thong of a whip, when I heerd a miserable louster up in lote."—I was in the stable, sitting on the oat bin, plaiting the thong of a whip, when I heard a great noise in the loft above.

BREN CHEESE. Bread and cheese.

"Let's hay a bit o' bren cheese, you."

BRET OUT. Corn very dry at harvest time, so that the grains fall out of the ears or husks, is said to "bret out."

BREYAVE. Brave, fine, or good.

"Goo and galley the ducks out o' gearden, there's a breyave bwoy."—Go and drive the ducks out of the garden, there's a good boy.

BRICK REEL. A brick kiln.

BRISH. A brush.

"Hanner, Hanner, hast thee bolted the shoe brishes? I can't vind 'em."—Hannah, Hannah, have you swallowed the shoe brushes? I can't find them.

BRISH OVER. To jump nimbly over anything, as a gate.

BROCKS (*A.S. brecan*, to break). Fragments or scraps of victuals.

"Wull ye hay zomethin to yet? But there, we onny got a vew brocks left from dinnertime to offer ye."—Will you have something to eat? But we have only a few fragments left from dinner to offer you.

BROODY. A hen wanting to sit on her eggs is said to be "broody."

BROOKLIME. *Veronica beccabunga*, water speedwell.

BRUCKLE. Brittle.

BRUSSELLS. Bristles, the hair of a pig.

"I met wold Cooke tother day, comen up vrom shore wi' a gurt thornback in his hand. 'Ah!' a zed, 'I be mortal fond, you, of a good thornback.' 'Well,' I zays, 'I don't keer vor sich things; gimme a good bit o' brussell-back, that's the tackle vor me.'"

BUDGE. To stir, to move.

"I can't budge 'en a inch."—I can't move him an inch.

BUFFLE HEADED. Thick headed, stupid.

"He's a gurt zote buffle headed sort o' feller."—He's a great foolish, thick headed kind of fellow.

BUGLE (*Lat. buculus*). A young or wild bull. A common sign of inns in the Island, and seldom to be seen elsewhere. The bugle, or wild bull, was the supporter to the arms of Henry Beauchamp, Duke of Warwick, crowned King of the Isle of Wight by Henry VI. in 1443; and this probably was the cause of its adoption as a sign by the local vintners. At present, in most of the signs the bull's horn, or bugle, is substituted for the bull.

BULL'S EYES. A coarse sweetmeat, made of boiled sugar flavoured with peppermint.

BUNCH. A swelling caused by a blow.

BUNDLE OUT. To turn out, to start anyone off quickly.

"Come, look sharp, bundle out here!"

BUNNY. A small covered drain, or culvert, generally in front of a gate at the entrance to a field.

BUTT. A small meadow, or enclosure of land, generally near the house; probably deriving its name from being used for archery practice in old times.

BUTTERVINGERS. A clumsy or unskilful person, who lets things fall or slip from his grasp.
"Hold on too'n, wold buttervingers."—Hold on to him, old butterfingers.

BWOY. A boy.

BWOYLEN, THE WHOLE BWOYLEN. The whole lot or number, all of anything.
"The hool bwoylen lot on 'em vlow out o' doors."—The whole of them ran or rushed out of doors.

C.

CAA. To chatter or cry like a rook or jackdaw.

CAG. To insult, to offend.
"I've ben and cagged en now, I louz."—I have offended him now, I think.

CAGMAG. Bad or stinking meat; also, coarse, uncultivated, mongrel bred.
"I wouldn't hay sich cagmag in a gift."—I would not have such bad meat if given to me. "'Tes a gurt cagmag sort o' hoss."—'Tis a great mongrel bred kind of horse.

CALL. Necessity, reason for.
"There's noo call vor thee to do that."—There's no necessity for you to do that.

CALLARDS. Leaves and sprouts of cabbage.
"I *do* like a bit o' bwoyled ham wi' zum callards."

CAMMICK *(A.S. camoc)*. Almost any plant with a yellow flower, as St. John's Wort, Ragwort, &c.; but properly Rest-harrow, *Ononis arvensis*.

CAMMICKY CHEESE. Cheese made from milk flavoured with rest-harrow, giving it a strong, rank taste.
"I went over to wold Drudge's wi' a looad o' faggots, and when I'd unloaded he axed me to hay zummut to yet and drink; but a onny gid me zome fousty bread dree weeks wold, and a bit o' wold cammicky cheese. I couldn't show to't, zo I come away and left it; a med yet it hisself if a likes."

CAPPENDER. A carpenter.
"I'll zing you a new zong, that layetly has ben maade;
'Tes of a little cappender, and of a pretty maade.
I have a vancy vor you, you goos zo neat and trim;
But oh, my little cappender, what will become of him?"
—*Old Song.*

CAR. To carry.

CARKY. Vexed or annoyed.

CARRIAGE OF CORN. A load of ten quarters.

CASN'T? Can you not? Can't you?
"Casn't zee't?"—Can't you see it? "Why casn't doo't?"—Why can't you do it?

CAT'S CRAADLE (sometimes SCRATCH CRADLE). A game played with string by children.

CAVIL. Refuse of wheat after threshing, used as food for horses.

CHAW. To be sulky, to be continually naggling or complaining.

CHACKLE. To cackle as a hen.

CHAM. To chew, to cogitate sullenly or morosely.
"The pigs a ben and chammed my smock frock all to pieces."—The pigs have chewed my smock frock all in holes. "He keeps on chammen on't over."—He is continually ruminating on, or bringing some annoying thing to mind.

CHARM. People talking confusedly together; a loud chattering of persons or fowls.
"'Twas jest like a butter market charm."—'Twas just like confused and mingled sounds of the butter market. "Don't they fowls kick up a charm."

CHEESES. Seeds of the mallow (*Malva Sylvestris*), often picked and eaten by children.

CHEERUP. To chirp, to cry as a young bird.

CHEQUERS. The game of draughts.

CHID LAMB. A female lamb.

CHILLBLADDER. A chilblain.

CHILLED. Cold.
"I sim quite chilled."—I feel quite cold. "To take the chill off anything."—To slightly warm any liquid, to place anything for a short time by the side of the fire.

CHIM. The projecting rim of the head of a cask or barrel.

CHIMBLEY. A chimney.

CHINE (*A.S. cyne*, a chink). A cleft or ravine in the cliff, formed by the action of running water; as at Shanklin, Blackgang, Brooke, and other places in the Island.

CHINKERS. Chinks, fissures.

CHIPPER. To speak rapidly, or in an excited manner; also, to be impertinent.

"I heerd 'em chipperen."—I heard them talking. "Don't let's hay nooan o' yer chipperen here."—Don't let us have any of your impertinence.

CHITLENS. The entrails of a pig, cleaned and plaited together.

CHIVY. To chase or pursue anything.

"We've had a fine chivy aater'n."—We have had a fine chase after him.

CHIZZLE. To cheat or swindle.

"He chizzled me out on't."—He swindled me.

CHOCK. To choke.

"I be zo dry, I be prid near chocked, you."—I am so thirsty, I am nearly choked.

CHOCK-DOG. Isle of Wight cheese; or any eatable, very hard or tough. Isle of Wight cheese—sometimes called "Isle of Wight Rock"—is made from skimmed milk, and by keeping becomes exceedingly dry and hard. It is related that a cheese being sent to someone at a distance as a present, the recipient, not for a moment suspecting it was anything meant to be eaten, with great difficulty cut a hole through the middle of it, fitted it up, and used it for a grindstone with success.

"Wold Jem Cooper over at Brison went one day on a arrant to Yafford, and when a was there Missus axed 'en if a would hay a bit o' bren cheese and a drap o' beer. 'Iss, I wull, thenk'ee missus,' zays Jem; zo they brought'n zome bren cheese and beer; but Jem zet and looked at it, and ded'nt offer to begin. 'What's the matter, Jem?' zays Missus, 'ye got what ye wants, han't ye?' 'Noa, not quite, missus,' zays Jem, 'I wants the billhook to cut the cheese wi'.' Jem never got noo bren cheese there noo moore aater that."

CHOPPEKIN. The chap, or under jaw of a pig, salted and smoked.

"I minds 'twas one Vriday when wold Lilly come about the clock, cause we had a choppekin that day vor dinner."

CHUB, or CHUBBY. A small freshwater fish, the miller's thumb or bull-head.

CHUCKLEHEADED. Stupid, thick headed.

"What bist about there, chucklehead?"—What are you doing there, chucklehead?

CHURN. The entrails of a calf.

"I be gwyne to Athervell to git a caave's churn to-morrow."

CLAA. To seize or take hold of anything.

"Claa hold on't, you."—Catch hold of it. "I claad hold be 'en by the collar."—I seized him by the collar.

CLAMS. A kind of vice or wooden pincers, used by shoemakers and saddlers, to hold the leather between their knees while sewing.

CLAPPER-CLAA. To scratch.

"The wold dooman ded clapperclaa 'en proper."—The old woman did scratch his face well.

CLAP. To put or place.

"Clap it down there, you."—Put it down there.

CLAP. A half-door, a trap-door, the shutter of an unglazed window in a barn or stable.

"Open the clap, wull'ee; I wants to putt the haay up in lote avore rack-up time."

CLAP KNIFE. A clasp knife.

CLAPS. A clasp.

CLEEAN. Clean; also quite, entirely.

"He drowed a stooan cleean droo winder."—He threw a stone quite through the window.

CLEM. St. Clement, the tutelar saint of the blacksmiths, commemorated Nov. 23rd.

"The blacksmiths be gwyne to keep up Clem to-morrow night, you; they've zended to Yarmouth vor a pound o' powder."

On the evening of Nov. 23rd, "Clem" was kept up by the blacksmiths and their friends "firing" their anvils, till all their "powder" was expended, when an adjournment was made to some neighbouring alehouse, and the day was concluded with songs and festivity.

CLENTED. Clinched, as nails.

CLICK. To tick, as a watch.

CLIDERS. Goosegrass.

CLINK. A smart blow; also, to strike.
"Wold Jerry did jest about clink into'n."—Old Jerry did beat him smartly.

CLINKERS. Refuse, cinders, &c., of a blacksmith's forge.

CLITTERBALLS. Pieces of mud or clay sticking to the hides of horses.

CLOT. A clod.
"He took up a gurt clot and flung at me."

CLOUT. A blow.
"I'll gi' ye a clout in the head, my nabs, when I meets wi' ye." "Ye'll git yer years clouted predney, ye young wosbird."

CLUTCHED UP. Sitting very close in a corner.

CLUTCHED HIN. A hen sitting on eggs.
"I zay, you, our Dick's ben and vell into the sheepwash, and come hooam all drillen wet. A won't show to noo vittles, and a zets hunched up in chimley corner like a wold clutched hin."

CLUTTERS. Part of the tackling of a plough or harrow.

COATHE (*A.S. cothu*, disease). A disease of the livers of sheep, from feeding on wet lands.
"That sheep's coathed, I can zee."

COB. To beat anyone on their posteriors. This jocular punishment is seldom used but during hay and harvest time, when for some offence against the rustic code—such as helping himself to more food than he can finish, or drinking more than his proper allowance—one of the labourers is sentenced to be "cobbed" by his fellows, who are both judges and executioners. The culprit is seized, and held in such a position as to fully expose his buttocks to castigation, which is generally administered with a boot,—six or twelve blows being given, according to the gravity of the offence.

COBNUT. A large kind of filbert, or any large nut.

COCKSETTLE. To turn head over heels, to throw a somersault.

COMPOSITION. A material used by bakers instead of yeast.

COOKEY BAABEY. The arum; sometimes called "Lords and ladies."

Coop. A prison.
"He's in coop."—He is in prison.

Cotterul. The hook to which the pot or kettle is hung over the fire.

Count. Worth, importance.
"He's noo count at all."—He is of no importance, not worth consideration.

Couch. Creeping wheat grass *(Triticum repens)*, collected in heaps and burnt.

Cowlick. A tuft of hair on the forehead, which will not lie in the same direction as the rest of the hair.

Craa. The craw or crop of a bird; the bosom or stomach.

Crapzick. Sick from over eating or drinking.

Craydel. A bow of wood or iron fixed to the snead of a scythe, to lay the swathe regular.

Crib. A child's bed; a receptacle for the food of cattle.

Cricket. A small three-legged stool for a child.

Crousty. Morose, ill-tempered, crabbed.
"The wold man sims terbul crousty this mornen."—The old man is very ill-tempered this morning.

Cruckle. To bend or stoop in walking, to hobble.
"There goos wold Bucket, crucklen along wi' two sticks."

Crumpled. Crooked; also, rumpled or creased.

Crumplen. A small apple, with a wrinkled rind.

Cuckoo spet. The white froth on leaves, covering the larva of the *Cicada spumens*.

Cue. The semicircular piece of iron on the heel of a boot.

Cummy. Bread turned mouldy, in hot weather generally.
"The poor bwoy was maade to yet cummy bread, till the dust vlow out o' the corners of his mouth when a chowed it."—The poor boy was forced to eat mouldy bread, till the dust flew out of his mouth as he chewed it.

Cup. A cry to bring cows home.

Cutten knife. A large triangular shaped knife, used with both hands, to cut hay from the rick.

Cutty. The Kitty wren *(Troglodytes vulgaris)*.

D.

DAA. A jackdaw.

DAB. A blow; also, to stick, or smear anything.

DABSTER. An adept, a proficient, a skilful person.
"You're a dabster at it."

DACK. A blow or stroke; also, to touch or stroke gently, to anoint.
"I'll gi' thee a dack wi' the prongsteel if thee doesn't mind."—I'll give you a blow with the prong handle if you don't take care. "My vinger is miserable bad, missus; jest dack en vor me, wull'ee."—My finger is very painful, missus; just anoint it for me, will you.

DAFFYDOWNDILLIES. Daffodils *(Narcissus)*.

DAPS. An exact likeness.
"She's the very daps of her mother."—She is exactly like her mother.

DARN. A kind of oath, a clarified d———n.

DEAD HOSS. To work on a "dead hoss" is to do work, the payment for which has been received and spent; to work out an old debt.

DEADLY. Very, extremely.
"I be deadly fond o' apple pudden, you."

DED. Did. "Ded'st?"—Did you?

DEFFER. To differ, to disagree.
"We agreed to deffer about that job."—We disagreed about that matter.

DENT. A hollow mark made in the surface of anything by a blow.
"That bwoy's ben an' dented the taabel wi' the hammer."—That boy has made a hollow on the table with the hammer.

DERECKLY MINNET. This instant, at once.
"If thee doesn't come down from therence dereckly minnet, I'll take a rice and drap into thee ready to cut thee all to pieces."—If you don't come down from there this instant, I'll take a stick and beat you very severely.

DESPURD. Very, exceedingly.
"That's a despurd good mare o' your'n, varmer."

Devil's dancen hours. Midnight.

"My wold man's gone to Nippert, and if there's a fiddle gwyne anywhere, I shan't zee'n hooam till the devil's dancen hours."

Devil's guts. The dodder plant.

Dewberry. The largest kind of blackberry.

Dewbit. A piece of bread and cheese taken by labourers early in the morning, before beginning work, in hay or harvest time, while the dew is on the grass, an hour or two before breakfast.

Dibble. To make holes for planting seeds or potatoes.

"I've jest dibbled my taeties in, you."

Dick. A game of touch-and-run among children.

Dido. A disturbance or row; an eccentric freak.

"He kicked up a middlen dido about it."—He made a great disturbance about it.

Dill. A word to call ducks.

Discoous. Converse, discourse.

"I dedn't hay noo discoous wi'en."—I had no conversation with him.

Dishwasher. The wagtail.

Dismolish. To destroy, to break in pieces.

Dock. The plant *Rumex*. Its leaves are sometimes used to wrap up fresh butter.

Dogged. Very, excessive.

"He's dogged cute, you."—He's very sharp, or knowing.

Dooman. A woman; generally preceded by "wold," as "my wold dooman."

Door darns. The side posts of a door.

Doughbaked. Silly, of weak mind, half-witted.

"He's a kind o' doughbaked sort o' feller."

Doughnuts. Round cakes about the size of a cricket ball, made generally of the same ingredients as a cake, but boiled in lard instead of being baked.

Dout. To extinguish, as a candle or fire.

Downarg. To contradict, to browbeat, to silence by overbearing assertions.

"He very nearly downarged me out o' my own neyam."—He very nearly argued me out of my own name.

Dowse. A blow; also, to splash, or throw water over anyone.

"If thee bisn't off sharp, I'll gi' thee a dowsen."—If you are not quickly gone, I'll throw some water over you.

Dowst. Dust.

Draa. To draw.

"Last Whit Monday aaternoon, you, I went into Nippert to zee a bit o' the Fair vor a nower or two; and I'd jest got auverright the Hare and Hounds when I zid a wold feller in a long smock frock at a stannen by the corner, a zillen cheese. A had a gurt rammel cheese under his yarm, and when a zid me stop a stuck a taaster into the cheese and holded it out agen me. 'Taaste,' a zays, 'wullee.' 'Noa I won't,' I zed too'n, 'thee onny wants to *draa me in*, but thee bisn't gwyne to.' Zo I zaamered downalong a little vurder, and went into the Lamb."

Drag. A large kind of harrow.

"We be gwyne draggen in zix acres to-morrow mornen."

Drap in. To beat, to strike.

"If thee doesn't mind, I'll drap into thee with the whip predney."—If you don't take care, I'll beat you with the whip presently.

Drangway. A narrow passage between two houses.

Dree. Three.

"I louz 'tes about dree o'clock, you."—I think it is about three o'clock.

Dresh. To thresh.

"We be gwyne to Buccombe this aaternoon aater the dresh machine."—We are going to Bowcombe this afternoon for the threshing machine.

Dreshel. A threshold.

"This gurt pig zays, 'I wants meeat;'
T'other one zays, 'Where'll ye lay et?'
This one zays, 'In gramfer's barn;'
T'other one zays, 'Week! Week!
I can't git over the dreshel.'"

—*A Nursery Jingle, used in catching or counting children's toes.*

Dretten. To threaten.

Drillen. Dripping with wet.

DRINE. A field drain.

DRINEN. Draining, the work of digging a drain.

DRIP. A trap to catch mice or rats. To "set a drip" is to take a piece of board about six inches square, and fix a nail in two opposite corners of it; then place this piece of wood (the drip) in the corner of a room infested by mice or rats, where two shelves meet, fixing it by the nails at the corners so as to make an almost perfect balance. A tub or large pan three parts full of water is placed directly under the *drip*, and the bait is put on the corner of the *drip* furthest from the wall. The rat or mouse, in trying to reach the bait, overbalances the *drip* and falls into the water beneath; and the *drip*, if properly set, falls back into its original position, ready for another victim.

DRO. To throw.
"Dro it down bout house."—Throw it down on the floor.

DROAT-HAPS. A leather strap that goes under the lower part of a horse collar, to hold the "*Haames*" together.

DRO IN. To carry sheaves together to be put in "hile" at harvest time.

DRUG. Damp or moist; also, heavy.
"That shower's made the haay rather drug, you." "Hollo, meyat! the roads goos deuced drug to-day, I sim."—Hollo, mate! the roads are heavy travelling to-day.

DRUSS. A descent in the road, or slight slope.

DRYTHE. Thirst, drought.

DUBERSOME. Doubtful, anxious.
"He sims terbul dubersome over it."—He seems very doubtful about it.

DUCKEST. Twilight, the dusk of the evening.

DUCKSTOOAN. A game played by boys, in which a small stone is placed on a larger, to be thrown at; and the first that knocks the stone off its support cries "duck," and is considered winner for that time.

DUFFER. A pedlar, or hawker of tea, cloth, or ready-made clothes, who sells "on tick," and calls on his customers about once a fortnight.

Isle of Wight Dialect.

DUMBLEDORE. A large humble bee.

DUNCH. Dull, deaf, hard of hearing.

"The wold man's got quite dunch lately."

DUNGMEXEN. A dunghill.

DUNGPOT. A heavy two-wheeled cart for carrying dung.

DUNNICK. A hedge sparrow.

DWYES. Currents, eddies.

E.

EATH or YEATH. Earth.

EACE. A large earthworm.

ELLUM. Elm; also, a handful or layer of straw, prepared for thatching.

EMMET. An ant.

"I zay, you, zummer's come,—here's a emmet."

EMPT. To empty anything, to pour out.

"Look sharp and empt the willey, meyat."

ETHER. A long flexible piece of underwood—generally hazel, making, when twisted or wattled round stakes, an *ether hedge*; also, a rod for chastisement.

"The wold man's aater'n wi' a ether."—The old man is seekfor him with a rod.

EVVET *(A.S. eféta)*. The eft or newt.

EX. An axle.

F.

FAGGED OUT. Very tired or weary, done up.

FAGGOT. A term of reproach or rebuke used to young girls.

"Come here, ye young faggot!"

FAIR DOOS. Fair dealing, equal or fair treatment.

"What cheer, you; how bist gitten on?" "Oh, I be middlen; how bist thee?" Oh, fairish, do'st know." "Have ye settled wi' Jobber Snow vor the shoots 'it?" "Well, not quite, you; I got to gi'n vour sacks o' tacties, and then 'twool be about fair doos booath zides."

FALL. The Autumn, the time of the leaves falling.

FEND OFF. To defend oneself, to keep anyone off.

FIGGY PUDDEN. A plum pudding.

FIRK. To be in a continual state of fuss or fidget; also, to scratch.
"That dog keeps on firken vor vlees."—That dog is continually scratching for fleas.

FIST. Progress, satisfaction, success.
"He'll never make noo fist on't."—He'll never have any success with it.

FITTEN. Right, suitable, proper.
"To my mind it don't sim fitten."—In my opinion it is not suitable.

FIT OUT. A commotion, a disturbance; an outcome or upshot.
"There was a fine fit out over it, you."—There was a great disturbance about it.

FLANYER. To flourish or brandish.
"He's out there by the barn door, flanyeren about wi' a sparrod."

FLEYAM. An instrument or lancet of an arrow-head shape, used to bleed cattle.

FLITCH. Wheedling, insinuating, plausible.
"He was terbul flitch wimme over it."—He was very insinuating, or wheedling, with me.

FLICK. The fat on the inside of a pig; a slight blow; an attempt or trial at anything.
"Let's hay a bit of flick to fry the liver wi'." "Gi' that hoss a flick wi' the whip, wull'ee you."—Give that horse a stroke with the whip, will you. "They be gwyne to plaay at vore corners vor a ham, at Braaden, Whit Monday, you; I louz I shall goo and hay a flick at it."—They are going to play at skittles for a ham at Brading on Whit Monday; I think I shall go and have a try at it.

FLICKEN COMB. A large-toothed comb.
Hannah was combing John's hair one Sunday morning with the "flicken comb," and, the hair being rather thick and matted together, the operation was too much for John's nerves, so he exclaimed, "Do stop, Hanner! doan't do noo moore too't! thee makes the vlesh crawl upon me booans."

FLING. To throw; also, to kick, as a horse.
> "Fling a stooan at'n." "Mind the wold mare don't fling at ye, meyat."—Be careful the old mare don't kick you.

FLOP. To fall down flat.
> "She come indoors and flopped down in a chair." "I vell down bout house flop."—I fell flat on the floor.

FLOWER KNOT. A small ornamental flower bed.

FLUE. The nap or down of anything.

FLUSTRATION. A scare or fright.
> "It putt me into a regular flustration about it."

FOGO. A disagreeable smell, a stink.
> "What a fogo! Drave that dog out o' doors."

FOOTEREN. Idling, trifling, busy about nothing.
> "He ben footeren about there dooen nothen all the mornen."

FOREST HOUSE. The House of Industry, or Workhouse for the Island, established 1770-75; so called from being built on land forming part of Parkhurst Forest.

> A labourer quarrelling with another said to him, "I'll tell'ee what 'tes, ye light-a-vire rogue, I sholl zee thee gwyne up Hunnyhill to Forest House one o' these days, wi' thee shoes down at heel."

FOREST HOUSE PUDDENS. Puddings made of flour and suet, which were supplied to the inmates of the "House" for dinner on Saturdays, and containing neither raisins, currants, nor sugar, were not held in much estimation. At a tumultuous meeting in favour of Reform held in the Corn Market, Newport, in 1831, some farmers from Gatcombe who were vehemently opposed to the popular cause were saluted with derisive cries, "Dree cheers vor the Forest House puddens." One of them in surprise asked, "Why be we Forest House puddens?" "Because ye ha'nt got no raisins (reasons) in ye" was the answer.

FOUSTY. Mouldy, mildewed, musty.

FRAAIL BASKET. A basket made of rushes, used by labourers to carry their food.
> "I zay, you, what's think? I jest met that gurt voreright Moll Young, trayepsen along wi' the mouth on her wide open, like a fraail basket hung up by one handle."

"You have pickt a raison out of a *fraile* of figges."—*Lilly's Mother Bombie*, 1632.

FRESH. Half drunk; also, new or strange.

"I zee varmer Lock's got a fresh keerter."—I see farmer Lock has got a new carter.

FUNCH. To push or thrust.

"Don't keep a funchen me zo."

FURRED-UP. Encrusted.

"This here skillet is all furred-up, missus.'

FURL. To throw, to toss anything over.

"I'll zend thee furlen if thee comes ancarst me."

G.

GAAK *(A.S. gæc)*. To look at anything eagerly; to stand and stare about in a silly manner.

GAB. Unnecessary or useless talk.

GALLANEY. A guinea fowl.

GALLUSES. Braces. " Gallus buttons."—Brace buttons.

"Come here, Betty, I wants thee to zow on one o' my gallus buttons vor me."

GALLY. To scare or frighten, to drive away.

"Tell the maad to gally the cows out o' rickus."—Tell the maid to drive the cows out of the rickyard.

GALLY-BAGGER. A scarecrow, a figure set up in a field to scare away the birds.

GAMBREL. A spreader; a curved staff, used by butchers to hang carcases on by the tendons of the hocks.

GAP. To jag or notch; also, a breach in a hedgerow.

"What a gurt gap he's maade in my knife!"—What a great notch he has made in my knife! "There goos the pigs, right over the gap into Vive Acres."—There go the pigs, through the breach in the hedge into Five Acres.

GARBED-UP. To be dressed in singular or uncommon manner.

"I was gwyne to Cheal last Zunday aaternoon, you, and 'long there by West Zide I run agen wold Spanner, garbed up like a wold gallybagger."

GAULLY. Thin or bad, applied to spots in a field where the crop has failed.

"That's a gaully piece o' wuts you got there, varmer."—That's a thin, or poor, field of oats you have, farmer.

GEARDEN. A garden.

"I be gwyne out in gearden to git zum callards vor dinner."

GEE (*g* hard). To give. Past tense—"gid."

"Take and gee'n zum on't."—Give him some of it.

GEE OUT (*g* hard). To give up, to knock under; to break by use.

"The keert rooap's gid out, meyat."—The cart rope has broken.

GEEAM LIG (*g* hard). A lame or diseased leg.

GEEAT (*A.S. geat*). A gate.

GENGE, or PLOUGHGENGE. The depth of the furrow.

"I must alter my genge when I gits out end."—I must alter the depth of the furrow when I get to the end of the field. "The raain cddn't gone into the ground not ploughgenge deep 'it."

GIDDYGANDER. The purple or meadow orchis.

GLOAT. To look intently, to stare.

"He gloats like a stuck pig."

GLUM. Dull, gloomy, out of spirits, sullen.

"The wold dooman es terbul glum this mornen."—The old woman is very sullen this morning.

GLUTCH. To swallow, to gulp down.

GOD A MIGHTY'S COW, or sometimes LADY COW. The ladybird, *Cocinella septem punctata*.

GOGGLE. Shaking, oscillating, tottering.

"That taabel is all of a goggle, missus."—That table oscillates or shakes, missus.

GOO. To go; also, the style or fashion. "Head goo."—The top or best.

"That's all the goo now." "That's the head goo on't all."—That's the best, or climax, of it all.

GOOSEBERRY WIFE. A large caterpillar, a bogey to deter children from picking the gooseberries.

"If ye goos out in the gearden, the gooseberry wife'll be sure to ketch ye."

GOOSEBERRY. "To play old gooseberry."—To make a great disturbance or commotion.

"If I tells meyaster I vound ye pinnen hes turmet greens, he'll plaay wold gooseberry wi' ye."—If I tell master I found you stealing his turnip greens, he will make it very uncomfortable for you.

GOOSEGOGS. Gooseberries.

GOOSER. An upshot, or end of anything.

"It's a gooser wi'n this time, I louz."—It's all up with him this time, I think. "If he don't git droo now 'twill be a gooser."

GOUND. A gown.

GRAAINS. Remains of malt after brewing, used to feed pigs.

GRABBLE. To snatch, or grasp roughly.

GRAFTER, or GRAFTEN TOOL. A spade of concave shape, used in digging drains.

GRAMMER. An old woman, a grandmother.

GRANDFER. A grandfather.

GRANDFER LONGLIGS. A large fly, or gnat, with long legs and wings, of the class *Diptera*.

GREEN LINNARD. A green linnet.

GRIP *(A.S. gripan)*. A handful of wheat newly cut.

GRIPPEN. Binding wheat into sheaves.

"All our vokes be up in Pound Close grippen, this aaternoon; there's nobody at hooam but missus."

GRISKEN. A fresh pork steak.

"We be gwyne to kill our pig a Friday, and we shall hay zum grisken vor dinner Zunday, you."

GRIST *(A.S. grist)*. Corn sent to the mill for grinding, and the flour which comes back.

GROANEN TIME. The time of a woman's accouchement.

"I louz 'tes groanen time wi' 'em at Duckmoor, you; the keerter told me missus expected to fall to pieces this week."

GROUND. A field.

"Where's ben to, you?" "Oh, I ben out in the ground aater the roller."

GROUND ASH. An ash sapling, growing from the ground.

GRUB. Food, eatables, victuals.

"Let's hay zum grub, missus, as zoon as ever ye can, vor I be as hungered as a hoss; I veels quite lear."—Let us have something to eat, missus, as quickly as you can, for I am as hungry as a horse; I feel quite empty.

GUDGEONS. Round pieces of iron fixed in the ends of a roller, by which it runs in its frame.

GUMPSHUN. Ingenuity, common sense.

GURT. Great.

H.

HAAIN UP. To preserve or lay up grass land.

HAAM *(A.S. healm)*. The stalks of plants, the haulm; as, "bean haam," "pease haam," "taety haam," &c.

HACKER. To stammer.

HACKLE (*A.S. hæcele*, a cloak or mantle). The feathers of a cock's neck; the straw roof over a bee hive. "To show hackle."—To prepare, or to be ready, to fight; from a cock erecting his "hackle" or neck feathers when about to fight.

HAGLETS. Icicles.

HAGGLER. One who buys poultry and eggs, to sell again; an upper farm servant, who looks after his master's horse, and the stock on Sundays.

HAMMER AND TONGS. "To go at it hammer and tongs."— To quarrel or fight furiously.

HAND. A part or share.

"I was toold he had a hand in it."

HANDS. Men, assistance, or help.

"Tell meyaster we wants zum moor hands, else we shan't top up the wheeat rick to-night."

HANDSEL *(A.S. handsyllan)*. The first money taken in the day, or for the first part sold of anything.

HANDY. Skilful, clever; also, close or near to.

"Plumley es a very handy wold feller." "I louz 'tes handy one o'clock, meyat."—I think it is nearly one o'clock, mate. "Putt the ladder handy to me, wull'ee you."

HANDSTAFF. The handle of a flail, to which the "zwingel" is fastened by a thong.

HANG-GALLUS. Fit for the gallows; one that ought to be, or is likely to be, hanged.

"Oh, he's a hang-gallus rascal."

HAPETH. A halfpenny's worth.

"That chap's a bad hapeth."—That fellow is good for nothing.

HAPSE *(A.S. hæps)*. A hasp.

HARD. Strong, big.

"He's a gurt hard bwoy."—He is a big, or strong, boy; "hard" being the opposite of tender in a child.

HARD DOES. Hard or bad times.

"'Tes miserable hard does wi' 'em, you."—It is very bad, or poor, times with them.

HARD PUDDEN. A pudding made with flour only, and boiled and eaten with meat.

HARL. To be knotted or entangled; also, a general confusion.

"The keert rooap es all harled up."—The cart rope is altogether entangled. "I went over to Tinker's Laane yesterday to gi' Jim a spell vor a vew hours, and I never vound things in sich a harl in my life: he'll make a purty zet out on't avore a done wi' et."—I went to Tinker's Lane yesterday to relieve, or help, Jim for a few hours, and I never found things in such a confusion in my life: he will make a pretty mess of it before he finishes it.

HARLENS. The hock joints of a cow or heifer.

"The wold cows got stuck in the keert loose up over their harlens."—The old cows got stuck in the cart ruts above their hocks in mud.

HARPEN. To be continually talking on one subject, to importune, to pester.

"She keeps on harpen me vrom mornen to night."

HASH. Hasty, impetuous, severe.

"Don't ye be too hash wi' that colt."

HASLET. The liver, lungs, and heart of a pig.

HASSICKS. Tufts of coarse grass, rushes, or sedges.

HATCH. To tear or slit anything by catching it on a nail, or some projecting object.

"I've maade a middlen half hatch in my breeches, meyat, gitten over that wattle hurdle."

HATCH ON. To yoke horses to the plough or harrow, &c.

HATCHED UP. To be walking arm-in-arm, as a courting couple.

"A Zunday a two ago I was out at Whiteley Bank, you, and I met Bob Smith and wold Tom Cooper's maade, gwyne along hatched up, and looken as zote as two gurt mud caaves together."

HAY. Have.

"Let's hay't, you."—Let me have it." "Will ye hay a bit o' bren cheese?"—Will you have some bread and cheese?

HEADLEN. Headland, the part of the field nearest the hedge, at the ends of the furrow, where the horses turn in ploughing.

HEAL *(A.S. hélan).* To cover. To "heal in" corn or potatoes—to cover them with earth; to "heal in" a rick or house—to cover it with thatch, &c.

HEELTAPS. Liquor left in the bottoms of glasses after drinking.

"Don't leave noo heeltaps."—Empty your glasses.

HEFT. Weight; also to lift anything, so as to try the weight of it.

"Jest heft it, wull'ee you."—Just lift it, so as to feel the weight of it.

HET. To hit; also, heat.

"Hullo, mayet, thee looks prid near shrammed, casn't ketch het this mornen?"—Hullo, mate, you look very cold, can't you get warm this morning?

HEYAMS. Pieces of wood fitted to the collars of horses, with staples to which the traces are fastened.

HEYATH. The hearth, or fireplace.

HIDEN. A beating.

"Won't I gi' thee a hiden when we gets hooam."

HIGHTY TIGHTY. An exclamation, generally used to naughty children.

"Highty tighty, two 'pon a hoss, what be ye squinnying about here."

HIKE OFF. Begone, be off with you, used generally in a contemptuous sense.

HILE. A double row of sheaves, generally 12, set up in the field ready for carting.

"The wheeat in Corner Close es all up in hile."

Ho (*A.S. hogian*) To long for, to be anxious; also, to be cared or provided for.

"I don't ho vor'n, I can tell ye."—I don't long for him, I can tell you. "'Tes a good job the poor wold dooman's hoed vor now."—It is a good thing the poor old woman is cared, or provided, for now.

HOBBLE. Trouble or difficulty; also, to tie the legs of an animal to keep it from straying.

"He's got hisself into a pretty hobble."—He has got himself into great trouble.

HOBLERS. Sentinels or watchers at beacons, in the Island, mounted on hobbies, or small horses, whose duty was to give the alarm on the approach of an enemy.

HOBNAILS. Broad-headed nails for boots.

"When I used to be Haggler at Athervell farm, there was a gurt bufflehead chap about there that used to go vor arrants, we used to call'n 'Traykleheact.' A was gwyne into Nippert one day, and Missus zed to'n,—'Goo into Way's and bring me zix poun of cracknels back wi' ye.' Well, by the time 'Traykleheact' got into town, he couldn't mind where he had to goo vor the cracknels, zoo he goos into a iremonger's, and axed vor zix poun o' *cracknails*. The man looked at 'en and zays, 'We don't keep noo nails of that naame; do ye mean *hobnails?*' 'Noa,' zays Traykleheact, 'she zed *cracknails*, but I spooase t'others 'll do, zo let's hay zix poun on em.' Bimeby back a comes, and zays, 'I zay Missus, they hadn't got noo *cracknails*, zo I brought ye zix poun o' *hobnails*; I louz tes anewse the saame thing.'"

HOCKS. Feet.

"Don't putt thee gurt hocks up agen me."

HOG. A sheep a year old.

HOGAILS. The berries of the white thorn.

HOLD WI'. To side or agree with, to support an opinion.

"He holds we the hare, and runs we the hounds."

HOLDVAST. A word used in the hay and harvest field, as a signal to the horses to move on, and for the man on the load to hold on.

HOOAM HARVEST. A farm supper and merrymaking at the end of harvest.

HOOAST. A host, a large number.
"There was a hooast o' people yesterday at the cricket match at Hulverstone."

HOOK. To strike or gore with horns, as a cow or bull.
"Mind the wold cow don't hook ye." "Hook out."—To pick or draw out anything from a crevice or shell.

HOOPIE. The game of hide and seek played by children.

HOPED UP. Perplexed, troubled.
"She es terbul hoped up over it."—She is very much perplexed or troubled about it.

HOSS. A horse.
In a team the shaft horse is the "thiller," the next before him the "body hoss," then "lash," "next to vore," and the first, the "vore hoss." "They don't sim to hatch hosses together noohow."—They don't at all agree or coincide in opinion.

HOSS STINGER. The dragon fly (*libellula*).

HUFF. To breathe hard, to puff and blow.
"Gwyne up hill makes me huff."

HOT. Hasty, passionate.
"Ye can't zay a word too'n, but a gits as hot as a Brisoner" (*i.e.* a native of Brighstone).

HULLS. The husks and refuse of corn after winnowing, used to feed horses; wheat hulls are the best for fodder. "Wut hulls" are sometimes used instead of feathers for beds.

HUNCHED UP. Shrunk in size, shrivelled; also, shrinking or cowering.
"A zets by the vire, nose and knees together, hunched up like a bundle o' wold rags."

HUNK. A large solid piece of anything eatable.
"I cut 'en off a gurt hunk o' pork and bread, and a zet down and scoffed the lot in vive minutes."—I cut him off a large piece of pork and bread, and he sat down and ate it in five minutes.

HURDLE SHELL. Tortoise shell, generally used of colour.

"I zay mayet, talk about cats, I got zummet like one now, a hurdle shell one, you. I war'nt she es a good one: she'll ketch birds and yaller hammers; but the wust on her es, I vound her up top o' taable in the dish o' pork and turmet greens left there over night, when I come down stairs in the mornen. I up wi' my skitter boot and let drave at her, and het her sich a clink by the zide o' the head, and knocked her down as dead as a rat; she onny went kick, kick, a vew timos, and never moved a wag aaterwards; but when I come hooam at night, there she was, zetten avore the vire as if nothen was the matter we her."

I.

IDLE. Saucy, wanton, flippant.

"That maade is jest about idle: she wants taken down a peg or two."

IGG. An egg.

INN. To enclose, now almost obsolete.

"The first part of Bradinge Haven wase *inned* by Sir William Russell, owner of Overland, at ye tyme when Yarbridge wase made."—*Oglander MSS.*

INNERDS. Entrails.

"Varmer Dore's gwyne pig killen to-morrow, and we be gwyne to hay one o' the pig's innerds."

INYUNS or INEYUNS. Onions.

IRE. Iron.

"Pick up that bit o' ire under hedge there, mayet."

IT. Yet.

"Es it one o'clock it, you?" "He eddn't vive year wold, nor it near."—He is not five years old, nor yet near it.

As an example of the antiquity of some of the provincialisms used in the Island, and how little they have changed,—in the MSS. of Sir John Oglander, written over 250 years ago, "*it*" is invariably used for *yet*.

J.

JAA. A jay, sometimes called "pranked jaa."

JAANT. A journey, a long walk.
"The pigs got out o' the ground into the road, and went all up to Blackdown. I've had a middlen jaant aater 'em: I can hardly wag."

JACK-A-LANTERN.—Will o' the wisp, the *ignis fatuus*.

JACKASSEN ABOUT. Occupied with trifles, busy to no purpose.
"I went down to Mill aater the grist, and 'twuddent ground, 'cause there was noo water; and then I went over to wold Brown's to zee if he had rung the keert wheels, but he was gone to Rookley, shooen; zo I ben jackassen about like that all the mornen."

JACKDAA. A jackdaw.

JACKHEYARN. A heron.

JACKRAG.
"Every jackrag on 'em's gone, you."—Every single one of them is gone.

JANDERS. The jaundice.
"I met we wold Gladdis last Monday, you, and a toold me his wold dooman had the yaller janders miserable bad."

JAW. To scold, to find fault with, to naggle.
"I must be off hooam, else I sholl git a middlen jawen."— I must be off home, or I shall get a good scolding.

JEE. To fit, to agree, to get on well together.
"They don't sim to jee together noohow."—They don't get on well, or agree together at all.

JEEAD. A jade, an old mare.

JEST ABOUT. Very, extremely, completely.
"He jest about ded slip into 't, mayet."—He did go at it, or into it, vigorously. "He jest about es a gurt feller, I can tell'ee."—He is a very big fellow, I can tell you. "Wold Warder danced a hornpipe in the Vive Bells t'other night, and a ded it jest about well."

JIFFY. In a moment, a very short time.
"He was off in a jiffy."

JIPPER. Juice, or syrup of anything, as of a pudding or pie.
"Mind what thee bist dooen wi' the skimmer, thee'st lat all the jipper out of the pudden."

JOBBER. A cattle dealer.

JONNICK. Fair, all right, as it should be, trustworthy.
"He acted very jonnick about it."

JOLTERHEAD. A heavy, dull, or stupid fellow.

"When I used to be keerter at Messon, a good many years agoo now, I had a gurt jolterheaded bwoy vor mayet wi' me; a was a regular zotey. One day a was gwyne into Nippert vor zummet or nother, and wold meyaster zed too'n, 'Call in at buttcher Lock's and bring back a lig of mutton wi' ye.' Zo away a went and got t'other zide o' Blackwater, and then all at once a swealed round, a back a come as hard as a could pelt. 'I zay meyaster,' a zed, 'which be I to bring, a vore lig or a hind one?' 'Thee tell buttcher Lock what I zed to thee, and 'twull be all right,' zays wold meyaster, 'thee bist about as clever as Betty Moorman's caaf, what run dree mile to zuck the bull.'"

JORUM. A large cup or jug.

JOSKINS. West countrymen who come to the Island for work, at turnip hoeing time and harvest.

JOURNEY. A day's work at plough, or at anything else with a team of horses.

K.

KECK. To retch, or heave as if sick.
"That ere stuff makes me keck."

KECKHORN. The windpipe, generally of an animal.

KECKS or KEX. A dry stalk of hemlock or cow-parsley, sometimes pronounced "kecksy;" also, wild plums or sloes.
"'Tes as dry as kex, you."

KEEASKNIFE. An ordinary table knife.

KEEAVEN. Separating the corn after threshing from particles of straw, &c.

KEEAVEN RAKE. A rake with long teeth, used in "keeaven."
"We must slip into't, you, vor I wants to begin keeaven up."

KEEL. A kiln.

KEERT. A cart; also, to carry anything in a cart or waggon; to cart.

KEERT LOOSE. A cart rut.
"The heifers got stuck in the keert loose up to their harlens."

Kelter or **Kilter**. Order, condition.

"We be all in middlen kelter this mornen." "I zid Varmer Jaacob's team last Zadderday, you; he jest have got zome nice hosses now, and all in good kelter. He got a black un naamed Punch, he es a fine hoss, and a regular good un to pull."

Kettle cap. The purple orchis.

Keys. Pods, or seedvessels, of the ash, maple, or sycamore.

Kids. Pods of pease, beans, and vetches.

"My peas es out in kid fine, you." "Your beeans have kidded uncommon well."

Kindy. Rather.

"I sims kindy queer this mornen."—I feel rather unwell this morning.

King. Much, a good deal.

"It's a king better now than it used to be."

Kink. To twist or crease, to be entangled.

"The rooap es all of a kink."—The rope is all twisted. "Kinked up like a snake."

Kite boughs. The dead boughs of trees collected for fuel.

"I ben over to Coomley, you, and got a bundle o' kite boughs.'

Kissencrusts. The imperfect crusts of loaves which have stuck together in baking.

Kittle o' fish. A result, a mess, a bad state of affairs. (Properly *kiddel*, a dam or weir in a river to catch fish.)

"Thee'st meyad a pretty kittle o' fish on't."

Knap (*A.S. cnæp*). A small hillock, the brow of a hill.

Knittles. Strings for tying the mouths of sacks.

Knock off. To finish, or leave work.

"Hullo mayet, how d'ye like this weather? Blowed if it don't raain as if it hadn't raained avore this dree year." "Oi you, it don't stop to raain, it valls down; I shall knock off and goo hooam."

Knownuthen. Stupid, ignorant.

"He's a gurt voreright, knownuthen sort o' feller."

Kurn. To turn from flower to fruit.

"My appletrees have kurned very well this year."

L.

LAA. Law.

LAAYER. A lawyer.

LACK. To want or need.

LANTERN JAAS. The jaws of a thin, bony person.

LARBETS (*testiculi agnorum*). Larbets fried or in a pie, are, by some, considered a delicacy.

LARRAPEN or LERRAPEN. Loose made, shambling; also, a beating.

"Here comes wold Tom, larrapen along the road."
"Thee'st get a lerrapen, if thee doesn't look out."

LATTER LAMMAS. Behind and slow.

"He's a terbul wold fashioned latter lammas bwoy."—He is a very old fashioned, slow boy.

LARRANCE. An imaginary being, whose influence causes indolence; a pseudonym for laziness.

"I can't git up mayet, vor Larrance got hold on me."
"He's got Larrance on his back strong to day."

LAY. Pasture land, or recently mown clover field; also, relative positions of places.

"That's a nice bit o' clover lay there, you." "I knowed I couldn't be vur out, by the 'lay' of the country."

LEAZEN (*A.S. lesan*, to gather). Gleaning, after the wheat is carted.

LEBB. A calf's stomach; rennet, used in making cheese.

LEBB'N O'CLOCK. Eleven o'clock, an allowance of beer taken at that time of day, during hay and harvest time.

"Hollo mayet! 'tes about time to hay our lebb'n o'clock, edden't et?" "Oi you, let's hay the puncheon, and I'll tip it out."—Hollo mate! it's time to have our eleven o'clock beer, is it not? Yes, hand me the puncheon [a small keg] and I'll pour it out. "I worked one time, you, long wi' wold Ben Whillier down in Lingewood lower Brickyard. One Vriday when we got panid vor the month, we vetched zome beer vrom the New Inn, Shaaflet, and had zome on't; but we dedn't stop to drink it all then, but left a vore gallon jar vull till the next mornen vor lebben o'clock. Wold Ben had to stop in the keel all night to keep the vire up, zo we left the jar wi' he, and went hooam. Next day when we went vor our drop o' beer, we vound the jar outzide the keel, turned upzidown, zo we axed wold Ben where the beer was gone to. 'Well,' a zed, 'aater you was gone I had a rid herren vor me supper, and et maade me terbul drythy all night, zo I jest supped up that little drop ye left.'"

LED. Laid; also, a lid.
"Putt on the pot led: zee how the roke vlees out o' the pot."
—Put on the pot lid: see how the steam flies out of the pot.

LEDGERS. Rods fastened by "spars" to keep the thatch on a rick.

LEEF or LIEF. Soon.
"I'd as leef goo as not."

LEER. Void, empty, wanting food, a craving or empty stomach.
"I got up one mornen, and walked vrom Freshwater to Nippert on a leer stummick, you." "I louz tes ver' near dinner time: I veels quite leer."

LENCE. The loan of anything.
"I shall be glad to hay the lence o' yer bucket vor a nower or two, missus."

LEATHER. To beat, to thrash.
"Wold Squibb ketched me one time up in hes apple tree, and didn't he gim'me a leatheren: I han't forgot it vrom that day to this."

LEVVERS (*A.S. læfer*). The great yellow flag, or its leaves; the Iris.

LEVVER BASKET. A basket made of "levvers," or coar rushes.

LEW (*A.S. hleo*, shelter). Shelter from the wind, the *lee* side.
"I was zet down, you, the lew zide o' the hedge, and I heerd zomebody scuffen along the road, zo I looks droo hedge and zid twas wold Joe Sargent. A had zummet in his hand, zo I zays too'n, 'Hollo Joe! what's got there?'—'Oh,' a zays, 'I jest ben and ketched a faddikin.'"

LEWTH. A sheltered spot from the wind.
"Let's git into the lewth."

LEYACE. To beat.
"I've a good mind to leyace thee jacket vor thee."—I have a good mind to give you a sound beating.

LIBBETS. Rags, tatters.
"I tore my smock frock all to libbets gwyne droo copse."

LIG. A leg.

LIGHT-A-VIRE. An abusive term.
"Thee bist a reglar light-a-vire rogue, *that's* what thee bist."

LIMMER. Limp, pliable, easy to bend.

LIMLESS. All to pieces, smashed.
"Git out o' the way, or thees't be knocked limless."

LINCH (*A.S. hlinc*). A strip of copse, by the side of a piece of ploughed land, generally on the side of a hill.

LINNARD. A linnet.

LITTER. Straw. To "litter up."—To put the bedding under the horses for the night.
"Light the candle, mayet, 'tes pretty nigh half aater zeben, and let's goo and litter up."

LIVER AND CROW. Pig's liver, &c., fried; pig's fry.
"I zay you, don't the liver and crow smill jest about good, it makes my mouth water; 'tes about the best part of a pig I likes."

LOB TAW. A large marble.

LOCK. A small quantity of hay or straw, an armful.

LOGEY. Heavy, dragging, generally used of a burden.

LOLLOP. To walk in a shambling or lazy manner.

LONG. In consequence of, because.
"'Twas all long o' he that they done it."—'Twas because of him that they did it.

LONG DOG. A greyhound.

LOP ZIDED. One side heavier than the other, all on one side.

LOR A MASSEY. Lord have mercy,—an exclamation of surprise or impatience.
"Well, Betty, how be ye? I was up your way last night, and looked in, but you wudden't at hooam." "Noa, I was gone to hear the paason lecter about planets and stars, and the world gwyne round like a top, and a lot more on't; but Lor a massey, I don't take it all in. For jest look'ee, and I'll tell'ee vor why. You knows we be here at Motson now: why, while be talken we should be over at Kingston, or Godshill, or zomewhere afore now, if the world keeps on gwyne round as vast as he zed it do. 'Twon't do vor me: I bean't quite fool enough it to believe all that."

LORDS AND LADIES. The *arum maculatum*.

LOTE. A loft over a stable.

LOUNDER. A swinging blow.
"I gid 'en sich a lounder, and beeat 'en down bout house."—I gave him such a blow, and knocked him down on the floor.

LOUSTER. A sudden loud noise.
"The door vell down wi' such a louster, et maade me jump."

LOUZ. To think, suppose, imagine, to be of an opinion.
"Deds't thee ax Jan about that ere, you?" "Iss, I ded, and a zed a louz 'tes about right now; and meyaster zed he louz 'twull do very well."—Did you ask John about the matter? Yes, I did, and he said he thought it was about right now, and master said he supposed it would do very well.

LUCK. A pool of water left among the rocks by the receding tide.

LUCKEY. Probably a corruption of "look ye;" also, morose, sulky.
"I zay, come here, 'luckey.'" "He sims to be luckey about zummet or nother."—He seems sulky about something.

LUG. To pull or haul.
"I claaed hold bee'n and lugged'n out on't."—I caught hold of him and pulled him out of it.

LUG. A pole in land measure, 5½ yards.

LUGWORMS. Worms used for bait in fishing.

LUMPER. To strike the foot against some obstacle, to stumble.

LUMPY. Heavy, weighty.
"That hamper es rather lumpy; jest heft'n."—That hamper is rather heavy; just lift it.

LURRY. Balderdash, loose talk.
"He ded goo on wi' zome pretty lurry, I can tell ye."

M.

MAA. The maw, or stomach of an animal.

MAAMOUTH. A silly talking, stupid person.
"There, onny look at her; ded ye ever zee sich a gurt zote, maamouthed thing as she es?"

MAD. Angry, in a rage.
"Dedn't the wold dooman git mad and yoppel at me."—
Didn't the old woman get into a rage and scold me.

MAG. A mark, or stake, to throw at; also to scold, or naggle continually.

MAGGOT. A whim, caprice, or fancy.
"The head on un es vull o' maggots."—His head is full of whimsies, or crotchets.

MAGGOTTY. Whimsical, crotchety, fond of experiments.
"What a maggoty feller that Will Chiverton es, you. He tarred his pig's back all over t'other day, cause a zed 'twud keep the raain out on 'en the better."

MAKE UP. To coil up, as a rope.
"Make up the keert rooap, you, avore it gits in a harl."

MALLARD. A male duck, or drake.

MALLISHAG. A large caterpillar, generally found in cabbage.
"I ben out in gearden to cut a cabbage or two vor dinner, but they be very near all spwiled, and vull o' mallishags."

MALLUS. The common mallow, *Malva Sylvestris*, often called "mash mallus," from being used for poultices.

MARE'S TAAILS. Light, streaky, flying clouds.

MARINERS *(Fr. merelles)*. A rustic game, formerly called *Nine men's morris*, and as old as the XVI. century (see Shakespeare, *Midsummer Night's Dream* ii. 2). It is played on a board by two persons, with nine pegs or stones each, and each player endeavours to place his pegs or stones, in straight rows of three, at the intersections of the lines on the board, without the intervention of any pegs of his opponent. The board is often seen cut in the lids of corn bins in stables, and formerly was sometimes found of larger size cut in the turf on the downs, by shepherds. "Fox and geese" is a somewhat similar game, but played with more pieces, and more intricate moves.

MARVUL. Marble, or a marble.
"Let's hay a geeam o' marvuls."

MAYET (mate). A common form of address; the carter's mate, or assistant.

"Hollo mayet, how bist gitten on?" "Oh tolloll, you, think'ee; how bist thee?" "Oh, I be all right up to now, mayet."

MED. May, or might.

"I med a ben there if I'd minded to."—I might have been there if I had cared to.

MEEAD. A meadow.

MEALY-MOUTHED. Plausible, deceitful, hypocritical.

"I can't come alongside that wold feller at all, he's too mealy-mouthed vor me."

MEN. An expletive of contempt or defiance.

"Thee bisn't gwyne to frighten me men, I beant afeared un thee."

MENTS, or MENCE (*A.S. myntan*, to make up, or form). Likeness, or resemblance, to represent.

"The bwoy mences like his father."

MERRY. The common black, or wild cherry *(prunus avium)*, probably from the French *merise*. "Merries" used to be very plentiful in the Island, and several places are now called " Merry gardens," in different parts of it.

MESH. A run through a hedge made by a hare; also, a marsh.

"When I was liven at Bowner, there used to be a feller called Salter out ver' near every day droo the winter wi' a gun, in the meshes round Yarmouth. A hardly ever done a day's work, for work and he vell out zoon aater a was born; except now and then a'd do a job vor wold Billy Squires. A had one o' these gurt long duck guns, and a was a very good shot; and when a putt zix or zebben baccy pipes o' powder into her, and a half-a-poun' o' shot, a'd kill everything a could zee in the meshes wi'in half-a-mile,—or that's the yarn a used to tell; but I dedn't bleeve a word on't, cause I knowed a always was a miserable liar."

METHER (come hither). The word for horses to turn to the left.

MEYASTER. Master.

MEXON *(A.S. mixen)*. A dung heap.

MICHE. To play truant.
"That bwoy han't ben to school to day; he's ben michen."
"Shall the blessed sun of heaven prove a *micher*, and eat blackberries?"—SHAKESPEARE: *Henry IV.*, Pt. I., ii. 4.

MIDDLEMUS. Michaelmas.

MIFF. An offence, a slight quarrel or coolness between neighbours. To be "miffed."—To take offence at anything.

MILLER. A white moth, which flies in the twilight or candlelight.

MILT (*A.S. milt*). The spleen of a slaughtered animal.

MIN. Men.

MIND. To remember.

MINTS. Mites, small insects in cheese.

MINTY CHEESE. Cheese full of mites.

MISERABLE. Much, very, extremely.
"They hosses yet a miserable lot o' corn last winter."—Those horses ate a great deal of corn last winter. "Dost thee know Will Baker, you? he's a miserable gurt feller." "Fine mornen, you, edden't it?" "Oi, you, but 'twas a miserable rough night; dedn't the wind blow! I thought my chimley was comen down." Sometimes feelingly pronounced—"*miserabble.*" "Hollo, you, how dost seem to beat up? I han't zid ye vor ever zo long." "Oh, I beant much on't; my faace ben terbul bad layetly; my teeth paains me zoo." "Ah, the toothache es *miserabble* bad, I knows that." "Oi, you, 'tes wuss than anything, I bleeve; and every now'n ten the wold stumps 'ill gee sich a jump, and prid near jump out o' me head."

MIZE. To ooze, or slowly discharge.

MOLL ANDREY. A merry Andrew, or mountebank.

MOLL WASHER. The water wagtail.

MONTH'S MIND. A good mind, or great inclination.
"I'd a month's mind to a knocked 'en down there and then."
"Month's mind" is a curious instance of a phrase dating from before the Reformation, surviving in common speech long after its original meaning has been forgotten. The "month's mind" were masses said at a month after the death of a deceased person, for the repose of his

soul; the word "mind" meaning memorial, or remembrance. A sermon of Bishop Fisher's, *tempore* Henry VIII., is entitled—"A mornynge remembrance had at the monthe's mynde of the most nobyl Prynces, Margarite, Countesse of Rychmonde and Darbye." The expenses of these services were suited to persons of all ranks, that none who desired them might be deprived of their benefit. In the Churchwardens' accounts of Abingdon, Berks, is the following, among other similar entries. "1556. Receyved att the buryall and monethe's mynde of Geo. Chynche XXIId." In the same year they received for the "month's mind" of the "goodwyfe Braunche, 12s. 4d." There were also year's, and two years' mind, observed.

MOONLIGHT BRANDY. Smuggled brandy.

MOOT. The stump of a tree left in the ground.

MOOT END. The stump, or tail end of a thing.

MORE. The grubbed up root of a tree.

MORGAN. The stinking camomile, *anthemis fœtida*.

MORTAL. Very, exceedingly, excessively.
"'Tes mortal hot to day, you, edden't it?"

MOTE. A small piece, a morsel.
"There edden't a mote on't left."

MOTHERY. Thick, applied to liquors, as beer, with mouldy particles floating in it.

MOUTHEY. Abusive, impertinent.
"He was terbul mouthey to me." "Shet up, mouthey! that's enough on't; we don't want nooan o' thy slack here, and I bean't gwyne to hay noo aaterclaps. I zold the rabbits to thee out and out, and thee'st hay to stick to 'em; zoo the best thing vor thee to do es to hike off hooam, or I med take zome o' the rine off on thee."

Mow. A stack in a barn, in distinction to one out of doors.

MOW-BURNED. Hay or corn put together before it is dry, and spoiled by heating.

MUCH. To stroke or pat, to make much of an animal.

MUCKEL. Refuse, or rotten straw.

Muck out. To turn, or drive, out.
"He was mucked out on't neck and crop, sharp."—He was turned out of it at once.

Mucker. All over with, finished, hopeless.
"I louz 'tes a mucker wi 'en this time, you."—I think it is all over with him this time.

Mud. A silly, thoughtless person; generally applied to a child.—"Ah, ye zote mud, don't do that." Also to pet, or cocker.—"Don't mud the bwoy up zo." A "mud calf" or lamb is one brought up by hand.

Muddle headed. Confused, bewildered, or stupid.

Muddled. Stupid, half drunk.

Mudgetty. Short, broken; as straw trodden by cattle.

Muggy. Moist, sultry weather.

Mum. A louse, or any small insect.

Mumchance. A shy or stupid person, who sits silent in company.
"A zet there mumchanced up in the corner, and never zed a word, good, bad, or indifferent, all the time a was there."

Mummick. To cut or carve food awkwardly or unevenly.
"Don't mummick that bread about zo; why casn't cut it fair?"

Mumpoker. A bogey, a term used to frighten or quiet children.
"If you don't gee off squinnyen, wold mumpoker 'ill come aater ye."

Mummy. The dusk, or twilight, in the evening.
"'Twas gitten mummy avore I come away, and 'twas zo dark I could hardly zee my hand avore me when I got to Apse."

Murren berries. The berries of the black briony.

Mwoilen. Working or toiling uselessly, to no purpose.
"If ye keeps on mwoilen there to Zatterday night, ye won't yarn yer salt."—If you keep toiling there till Saturday night, you won't earn your salt.

N.

Naaize. A noise; also a scolding, or disturbance,
"Ther'll sure to be a naaize about it."

NAB. To catch, or capture.

"He'll git nabbed one o' these days."—He will be caught some time or other.

"My nabs."—A kind of expletive used in conversation, almost untranslatable; a certain person, you, he, himself.

"Now, my nabs, I've got a booan to pick wi' you."—I have a complaint, or, I want an explanation from you. "I lost my cross axe a week or two agoo, you, and I zomehow fancied where wold Jem White hadn't got 'en; I knowed a was grubben a hedge vor Varmer Trell, zo I slips down along by the zide o' the hedge yesterday, and there I vound my nabs usen my cross axe. He zoon drapped'n when a zid me comen."

NAMMET. Refreshment taken in the hay or harvest field at four in the afternoon, consisting of bread and cheese and a pint of strong beer; the "nammet beer" being older and stronger than any supplied at other times of the day.

"I zay, you, chuck us my nammet bag over here, wull'ee."
"If we don't slip into't we shan't git the wheat in hile by nammet time, mayet."

NANNY A she goat; also, a prostitute.

NASHUN. Great, very, exceedingly; also, a mild kind of oath.

"'Twas nashun dark last night." "He's a nashun unbleeven bwoy." "Nashun saize you, git out o' the way!"

NEAR AS A TOUCHER. Very near, or close shave; a narrow escape.

NECESSARY HOUSE. A water closet, or privy.

NECK AND CROP. Altogether, entirely, completely.

NECKLE. A house, a dwelling.

NEDDY. An ass.

NEEDS. Forsooth, in consequence, to take an opportunity.

"Our keerter went to Cowes wi' a looad o' straw last week, and instead o' comen back as quick as a could, a must needs stop at the 'Hoss Shoe' vor a nower or two, and come hooam dree parts slewed."

NETTLE CREEPER. The small whitethroat.

NEWSE (see *Anewse*). "Newse" or "anewse the matter," nearly right, or as it should be.

Nineted (probably a corruption of anointed). Notorious, incorrigible.

"Don't hay nothen to do we that feller, he's a nineted rogue."

Night hawk. A night crow, the goat sucker.

Nit. Not yet.

"What time es it, you?" "Oh, 'tedden't one o'clock, nit near, it."—It's not one o'clock, nor near it, yet.

Nitch. A bundle of hay, straw, or wood; a burden, as much as one can carry.

"He can car a smurt nitch, I can tell'ee."—He can carry a large sized burden.

Nooan. None.

"Nooan on't."—Not any of it. "Nooan onts."—None of us.

Noo how. Out of order, in no regular shape, after no pattern.

"That rick is maade noohow."

Noo ways. Not at all.

"He's noo ways given to drink."—He is not at all inclined to drink too much.

Noo when. At no time.

Nor. None, not one.

"Es there ar one there, you?" "Noa, I can't zee nor one." —Is there one there? No, I can't see any.

Not (*A.S. hnot*, shorn, or clipped). Without horns, as a "not cow," a "not sheep."

Nother *(A.S. nather)*. Neither.

"You can't jump over that geat." "Noa, nor you nother."

Now-a-days. The present time.

Nub. A piece or lump of anything, as a "nub o' coal," "nub o' sugar."

Nuss tenden. Employed as a sick, or monthly, nurse.

Nut. The stock of a wheel.

"The waggon wheels got stuck in the keeart loose up to the nuts."

NUTTEN. A donkey.

"A wold man by the neyam o' Carben lived at Chessell, onny he's dead now; and a used to drave a donkey keert about, aater a got too wold to do any more work. One day, gwyne along the road out by Tapnell, a met wi' a team, and they drove the waggon right into the donkey and keert, and beeat the poor nutten's voot off, zo a had to be shot. The wold man was terbul putt out over it, but a thought a would goo to church the Zunday aater, vor a zed, 'I dare zay, now, the paason will praach about my poor wold nutten.' Now it zo happened that the lesson that Zunday was about Balaam and his ass, and the wold man *was* delighted. 'What a good sarmun,' a zed, when a got out o' church, 'I knowed the paason 'ud be sure to praach about my nutten, 'cause a was sich a good one.'"

O.

OBEN. An oven. "Oben rubber."—A pole with a cloth attached, to clear the oven of embers, before putting in the bread. "Oven peel."—A flat wooden shovel with a long handle, used to put in or take out the loaves from the oven.

ODD ROT IT. An exclamation of surprise or impatience.

ODDS. Difference, consequence, business.

"What odds es it to you where I goos to?"—What business is it of yours where I go to? "'Twull make no odds to me, let it be how 'twull."—It will make no difference to me, however it may be.

OFF. To be well or ill off, is to be well or badly provided or furnished with anything.

"How be ye off vor taties this year, you?"—How are you provided with potatoes this year? "Joe's bad off, but his brother is very well off."—Joe is poor, but his brother is in very good circumstances.

OI. Aye, yes. (The *o* pronounced like *au*).

"Prid near shet off time, edden't it, mayet?" "Oi, you."

ONE. Sometimes used for a.

"He kicked up the deuce o' one row about it."

OR ONE, AR ONE. One, ever a one.

ORE WEED. Seaweed washed on shore.

Our'n. Ours.
: "That staffhook under hedge es our'n, edden't it?" "Oi, you, I louz tes."

Out. To extinguish; sometimes, " dout."
: "Out the light, wull'ee, you."

Out at elbows. Offended, a disagreement.
: "They be all out at elbows now."

Overner, or Overun feller. A person whose home is over the water, on the main land; not a native of the Island. West countrymen, who come to work in the Island, are always "overun fellers," and regarded as foreigners by the natives. If they settle in the Island, gain any position, and are considered respectable, they are spoken of as "overun people."
: "Had a miserable rough night, you." "Oi, you, 'twas a reglar Luccomer, last night." "I wish it had capsized they there overners, comen across: what do they want over here, tryen to take the bread out o' vokes' mouths?" "If ar one on 'em zays ar a word out o' square to me you, I'll zwarm into'n pretty sharp, I can tell'ee." "Oi, you, that's the right way to sar 'em."

Overrods. The overhanging rails on the sides of a waggon.

Ovus. The eaves of a rick, or thatched building.

Paay. To pay; also, to requite, to beat.
: "I'll paay thee out vor that, my nabs, when I ketches thee."

Paddle. A small spade to clean a plough; also, to walk or trample about in the wet or mud.
: "There's that bwoy out doors, paddlen in the gutter: won't he make his clothes in a mess!"

Pank. To pant.
: "How that dog panks under the taable!"

Pansheard. A fragment or piece of a broken pan.

Peaked'. Pale or thin in the face.
: "She looks terbul peaked' to day."

Peeas haam. The stalks, or haulm of peas.

Peck upon. To domineer over, to keep under.
: "I was pecked upon all the time I was there, and used wuss than a dog."

PECKY AND MIMFY. Delicate, out of sorts.

"That maade ben terbul pecky and mimfy vor zum time."

PEER. Equal, comparable; also, to melt or clarify lard

"I never met we the peer too't."—I never met with its equal. "Tell missus to make a vew doughnuts; we be gwyne to peer the lard this evenen." (Doughnuts—which see—are boiled in lard).

PEEWIT. The lapwing.

PEGG OFF. To die.

"The wold man pegged off last night, you."—The old man died last night.

PELT. A skin, or hide; also, a violent rage, or passion.

"I broke the blaades o' the waggon, yesterday, and didn't meyaster git in a pelt about it, and show off at me."—I broke the shafts of the waggon, yesterday, and didn't master get into a passion and scold me.

Sometimes, also, quickness, or speed.

"I was looken vor a wire, when I zid the keeper comen athurt the ground, zo I jumps over hedge and went droo copse as hard as I could pelt: I was too many vor'n that time, you.

PEN UP. To shut up, or in; to confine.

"Goo and pen up the fowls, there's a good bwoy." "I sholl pen up that caaf next week, and begin fatten on 'en."

PICKEY BACK. To carry a child on one's back.

PIECE. A field of corn.

"That's a pretty piece o' wuts you got there, varmer."

PILL. A pitcher.

"I zended my Polly to Newbarn aater zum milk, and comen back she vell down and broke the pill all to pieces: I gid ninepence vor'n onny last week."

PIMPLE. A head.

"Han't a got a pimple on 'en, you! prid near big enuff to vill a willey."—Hasn't he got a large head! nearly big enough to fill a "willey" [which see].

PIN. To pilfer, to steal, to take clandestinely.

"Zomebody's ben down in orchard pinnen the apples." "Hollo, you! where did'st get they cowcumbers?"—"Oh, I pinned 'em, comen along the road this mornen."

PINCH. A crisis.

"It's come to the pinch this time, you."

PINCHERWIG. An earwig.

"I zay you, I left my clothes under hedge here, and now there's dree or vour gurt pincherwigs craalen about in my dinner bag; but I'll zoon settle their hash vor 'em."

PINEY. The peony.

PINNEY. A child's pinafore.

PIP. The *lues venerea*.

PISS-A-BED. The dandelion *(leontodon taraxacum)*, so named from its diuretic qualities.

PITCH. The quantity of hay or straw, &c., taken up at once with a prong; also, to put or throw up hay or corn into a waggon.

PITCH IN. To set about a thing at once, to go at it instantly.

"Pitch in, mayet, and let's git this job done."

PITCH UP. To stand and talk, to form part of a concourse.

"I started that bwoy aater zum barm, and a was gone zo long that I went to look vor'n, and as zoon as I turned the corner there a was, pitched up wi' dree or vour more, all yoppelen away at one another; but 1 zoon putt a stopper to that; they vlow round the corner like scalded cats when they zid me."

PITCHEN PRONG. A long-handled prong, a pitchfork.

"I spooas ye don't mind Jan White, the fiddler, what used to live at Moortown, in Brison parish;—but there, he was dead avore you was born. He was a miserable rum sort o' feller, and a used to zing in church one time. In the fall o' the year, one evenen, I was gwyne by his house, and 'twas raainen pitchen prongs wi' the vorks downwards; and there zet Jan on top o' the pig's house, in his shirt sleeves. 'Hollo, Jan!' zays I, 'whatever bist up to there?' 'Well, mayet,' a zays, 'I be tryen to ketch a good coold, zo I sholl be aable to zing base in church next Zunday.'"

PITZAA. A large saw used in a saw-pit.

PLAAY IN, and PLAAY SHARP. To begin at once, to strike in, to be quick or nimble.

"While t'others were footeren about, he plaayed in, and had it out in noo time." "Now then, plaay sharp, off wi' ye."

PLASH. To cut the branches of a hedgerow nearly—but not quite—off, bending them down on the bank, and partially covering them with sods, so that fresh shoots may be thrown out."

"I sholl have that hedge plashed next week."

PLATTER. A wooden dish, or trencher. Dishes made of pewter are usually called "pewter platters."

"We cleared off moost on't when we dinnered, you: 'twas vull bellies and empty platters."

PLIM. To swell, to expand in cooking.

"That bit o' pork'll plim in bwilen." "The ducks plummed up well in roasten."

PLOCK. A block, or log of wood.

"Let's putt a plock behind the vire, you."

PLUCK. The liver, heart, &c., of a sheep generally.

PLUNGE. To throb; a sensation of pricking or shooting.

PLY. To bend.

"I ben tryen to ply this bit o' ire, but I can't do't it."—I have been trying to bend this piece of iron, but I can't do it yet.

POCKMARKED. Marked with the small pox.

POKEN, or POKEASSEN, ABOUT. To go prying about; also, to fritter away time to no purpose.

POLEHAPS. A leather strap fastening the "haames" at the top of the horse collar.

POLLARD. Coarse bran; also, a trunk of a tree with the top cut off, sprouted again.

"I was gwyne athurt one o' varmer Starkes's grounds down at Flatbrooks one time, and I dedn't know the wold bull was there; but a was, and as zoon as a ketched sight o' me a was aater me vull butt. I could run middlen smirt then, but I had a hard matter to git out o' the way on 'en; however, I maade vor a pollard growen in the hedge, and climbed up into'n, and there I had to zet vor a nower or moore, till I was ver' near shrammed. The bull couldn't git at me, and I dedn't dare git down; vor a kept there, belven and tearen up the ground wi' his veet; till bimeby zome o' the chaps come along that had shet off, and was gwyne hooam to dinner. I zung out to 'em as loud as I could, and two or dree on 'em come over and beared in athurt mister bull with the paddle and a gurt ether, and maade 'en turn taail, or I louz I should had to bid there till next mornen."

E

POOK *(A.S. peac)*. To put hay or corn into heaps for carting. "Pooks."—Heaps of barley or oats, or hay-cocks.

POPPLESTOOAN *(A.S. papolstan)*. A large pebble.

POSTURE. To strike an attitude, to swagger.

"He was out posturen avore the winder jest to be looked at, maaken a reglar fool of hisself."

POT-LIQUOR. The water in which meat and vegetables have been boiled.

POWDEREN TUB. A tub to hold salt or pickled pork.

PRANKED'. Variegated, mottled, or speckled.

PRANKED' JAY. The common jay.

PRICKED. Sharp, slightly sour, as beer.

PRID NEAR. Very nearly.

"They prid near fout over it, you."—They nearly fought about it.

PRIDE O' THE MORNEN. A foggy, or drizzling, morning; often followed by a fine day.

PRITCHEL. A small hedge stake.

"That wold granny Burt was crapen down the road this mornen, picken up sticks, and I'm danged if she han't pulled every pritchel out o' my ether hedge. Dash her wold booans, I wish I'd ketched her at it; she wouldn't a vorgot et it awhile."

PROOF. Body, or fattening power, applied to food for cattle.

"There's zome proof in that clover haay, varmer."

PRONGSTEEL. The handle of a prong.

PROPER. Right, as it should be; also, very, exceedingly.

"That hoss is a proper good one to pull." "This tackle is about proper, mayet."—This eatable, or drinkable, is as it should be, or very good.

PUCKER. Trouble, vexation, perplexity.

"He's in a terbul pucker about it."

PUD. A hand, applied only to children.

"Come and warm your poor little puds, my dear."

Pudden headed. Stupid, silly, thick headed.

"Ded ye ever know wold Spanner, you? A used to live at the back o' the Island, at a plaace called Whisselgray, or zummut like it, handy Cheal. Hes wife was a terbul zoat, pudden headed zort o' woman, as thin as a rake; but there was noo harm in her. The wold man, you know you, had been bad vor a long time; zo one day a went into Nippert to zee the French doctor. The doctor zed to'n, 'You must take keer o' yerself, and drink jackass's milk the vust thing in the mornen, or else ye med git into a decline.' Zo a went off hooam, and toold his wife what the doctor zed. 'Dear, dear,' she zays, 'what a zet out! our wold Jenny don't gee no milk now, and I don't vor a minute think we sholl be able to git any.' 'Well, there, zays the wold man, 'the doctor toold me if I couldn't git noo Neddy's milk anywhere else, I was to come to'n agen, and he'd let me hay zome.' 'Lor a massy!' zed his wife, 'ye beant't never gwyne to zuck the doctor, be ye?'"

Pumble vooted. Club footed.

Puncheon. A small keg, containing from three pints to a gallon or six quarts; used to carry beer into the fields in hay or corn harvest time.

Punyear. To read or peruse a book.

"He's indoors, punyearen over a book."

Pure. Nice, good, well. "Purely."—Pretty well. (Not much used,—almost obsolete.)

Pur lamb. (A.S. *púrlamb*). A male lamb.

Purl. To turn swiftly round or over.

"He purled round like a top." "I putt a charge o' shot into'n, and a onny purled over a time or two, and never moved aaterwards."

Puss. A purse; also, the scrotum of animals.

Pussikey. A little, short, self-important, or conceited person.

"She's a reglar pussikey little bit o' goods."

Putt to. To be in a strait or difficulty, to be distressed.

"He's terbul putt to vor money jest at present."

Putt out. To be angry; also, to fret over misfortune.

"When I toold'n about it, he simmed a good deal putt out."

Putt up. To stop for refreshment, or take quarters for man or horse at an inn.

"Where d'ye putt up, you?" "Oh, I sholl putt up at the 'Green Dragon.'"

PUTT UP WI'. To endure, to bear patiently.

"I couldn't putt up wi'n noo longer, zo I gid'n the sack."— I could not bear with him any longer, so I discharged him. "When I got hooam last night, you, my wold dooman *was* cranky. She kep' on jawen me till I couldn't putt up wi' et noo longer, zo I started outdoors and left her."

PUTT UPON. To be imposed on, or domineered over.

"He's jest the sort o' feller to putt upon anybody under'n; but I'll look out he don't putt upon me."

Q.

QUAAITS. Quoits.

"He edden't a bad hand at quaaits: I be middlen, myself; but I can't come 'long side o' he."

QUAAM. A qualm.

QUARREL. A pane of window glass, properly diamond shaped. (Probably from the French *quarré*.)

"The lozange is a most beautiful figure, and fit for this purpose, being in his kind a quadrangle reverst, with his point upward like to a quarrell of glass."—*Puttenham*.

QUEAL. A quill; also, to coil or curl up.

"He was quealed up like a snake."

QUEAL IN. To go to bed.

"I be tired as a dog, and think I shall goo and queal in." "I zay you, I heerd yesterday that wold Joe Morris es dead, what used to live at Chillerton one time. He and his wife Nanny was a queer wold couple,—about the rummest vokes that ever I heerd tell on. One night in the zummer, aater they'd boath quealed in, it come on to thunder and lighten terbul heavy, and woke up wold Nanny, who was prid near frightened out of her wits; zo she rouses wold Joe up, and zays too'n, 'Joe, do let's git up! vor I raaly thinks 'tes the end o' the wordle, or the day o' judgment, come.' 'Bide quiet,' zays Joe, 'and let a feller sleep, can't ye, ye zoat wold fool; d'ye think the day o' judgment es comen in the night?'"

QUEER. Ill-tempered; also, to be sick or ill.

"If he acts anyway queer, I sholl start off hooam agen, sharp." "Hollo, Sam! how bist gitten on now?" "Well, I be better than I was, thinkee; but I have ben terbul queer vor the last week or two."

QUEER AS DICK'S HATBAND. To be in a very morose or sullen temper.

"I went over to Dogshaant last Monday, to zee varmer Morey about the keep vor the heifers; but zummet or nother had putt'n out. I could do nothen wi' 'en; he hardly spoke a dozen words to me, and was as queer as Dick's hatband."

QUERK. To sigh, or grunt.

"He goos about house querken like a wold zow."

QUID. To suck, to mumble in the mouth; applied generally to young animals.

QUIDDLE. To be fussy, or busy about trifles.

"He ben quiddlen about, doen nothen, all day."

QUILE. To coil; also, to quell, or subdue.

"They putt'n into a straight jacket, and that zoon quiled 'en."

QUILT. To beat; also, to cover a ball with a network of twine.

"I'll gee that bwoy a middlen quilten when I comes across 'en, for pinnen my plums."—I'll give that boy a severe beating when I meet with him, for pilfering my plums.

QUOT. To sit down, to squat.

"I quot down under hedge, and he went by and never zid me."

R.

RAA. Raw; also, a sore or tender spot.

"They hosses don't half pull together: titch Captain on the raa wi' the whip, bwoy."

RAAMES (*A.S. ream*, a ligament). The remains or fragments of a joint of meat, half-picked bones; also, a half-starved horse.

"'Tes Zadderday to-day, and we han't got nothen but a vew raames vor dinner; but there, we sholl cook to-morrow, beein' Zunday." "Wold jobber Snow wanted to zill me a hoss. I never zid sich a wold raames in my life: I toold'n I wouldn't hay 'en in a gift."

RABBIT. A mild kind of oath.

"Od rabbit the bwoy."

RACK. A barrier, or kind of hatch across the lower part of a barn door.

RACK UP. To fill the racks with food for horses or cattle, the last thing at night before leaving them.

"Come on, mayet, and git the cannel and lantern; we must begin to rack up, 'tes ver' near half-aater zeben, you."

RACKET. "To stand the racket" of anything.—To abide by, or to be answerable for, the consequences.

RACKETTY. Thriftless, extravagant, dissipated.

"He was a reglar racketty sort o' chap avore he got married."

RAFTY. Having a rancid, stale, or musty smell.

"That ham got a kind o' rafty smell wi' et; I can't stummick it."

RAMMEL CHEESE. Cheese made of new, or unskimmed, milk; the best kind of cheese.

RAMSONS. Wild garlic, *Allium ursinum.*

RAMSHACKLED. Old, dilapidated, broken, or out of repair; generally applied to an old crazy building, or vehicle out of order.

"He lives in a wold ramshackle plaace out at Lock's Green zomewhere." "I can't putt a hoss in sich a ramshackled wold keert as that; the zides 'ud vall out avore I got half-a-mile."

RANDY. Lewd, dissipated; also, a country fair or revel,—now almost obsolete in this sense, "Newtown Randy," the most noted of its kind, having been abolished for many years.

RAP AND RUN VOR. A saying.

"He'll never be wuth vive shillens, vor he spends all he can rap and run vor."—Only applicable to thriftless characters.

RARE. To raise or rear; also, to get into a violent rage.

"Rare up the ladder agen the rick, you." "Dedn't the wold man rare at me!"—Didn't the old man get into a rage with me.

RARE. Underdone, nearly raw; also, strong smelling.

RARRIDGE. A radish.

"I zay, goo out into gearden and git us a vew rarridges and a inyun or two vor zupper."

RATHE. Early; now almost obsolete.

RATHE RIPE. Early, or soon, ripe. In Northwood Churchyard is an epitaph on two children, who died in 1668 and 1670, which thus concludes:—
"Such early fruites are quickly in their prime,
Rathe ripes we know are gathered in betime;
Such Primroses by Death's impartiall hand
Are cropped, and landy'd up at Heaven's command."

RATTLEMOUSE. A bat.
"There's a gurt rattlemouse vleein' about in steyabel, you. Git the rudder, and let's ketch'n."

RATTLETRAP. An old worn-out vehicle.

RATTLETRAPS. Old and ricketty household goods.
"There's nothen in the house but a few wold rattletraps, not wuth a rap, and about half-a-bushel o' vlees."

RAZZER. A razor.
"Run in and ax your father to lend me his strap vor a vew minutes, wull'ee; I wants to strap my razzer, and sheeave this mornen avore dinnertime." "Here comes wold Bob Haazel, the razzer grinder, you: let's ax'n to grind our cutten knife; a wants sharpen bad enough."

"Wold Bob Hazel" perambulated the Island with his "razzer grinden" machine about 35 or 40 years ago; and one day, toiling along the road near Atherfield, was the subject of the second of the above remarks, made by the "keerter" to his "mayet," who were engaged in cutting hay from the rick with a "cutten knife" [which see], very blunt in the edge. As Bob was passing by he was accosted, and asked with a grin if he could grind the "cutten knife;" and to the surprise of his interrogators he coolly replied in the affirmative, took the knife, and commenced grinding it, making the sparks fly in showers, the pair of yokels watching his proceedings with some anxiety. When Bob had put the finishing touches to his work, he held out the knife with one hand, and demanded half-a-crown for the job with the other. The faces of the "keerter" and his "mayet" lengthened considerably on hearing this, as the sum was one which their combined purses could not supply; and Bob, seeing the cash was not forthcoming, put the knife on his machine and proceeded on his way leaving the discomfited pair staring in terror at the loss of the "cutten knife," and the consequences thereof when it came to the ears of "meyaster." Bob was scarcely half-a-mile on the road, when the required sum—by borrowing or begging—was obtained; and one of the circumvented tricksters, running after him, paid the half-crown, and, receiving the knife from the jubilant "razzer grinder," returned a sadder, and perhaps wiser, man.

REACHES. The ridges in a ploughed field.

READIED. Cooked thoroughly, quite done.

"The callards be cooked, missus; but the pork edden't readied enough it."—The cabbage is cooked, but the pork is not done yet.

READY. Nearly, almost.

"I've walked from Nippert all the way hooam; and I be zo tired, I be ready to drop."

REAREN. Raising or putting the roof on a new house.

"They'll have the ruff on at Appleford to-day, you: bean't you gwyne to the rearen feeast?"

'RECTUN POOAST. A directing or finger post. A favourite practical joke among the rustics, before the establishment of the County Constabulary, was to turn the "'Rectun pooasts" round, so that the arms pointed directly opposite to what they should do.

RENSE. To wash out, to rinse.

"Come on, you, and let's rense out these trendels."

RENYARD. A fox; Reynard.

"The next we zid was a blind man,
    As blind as he could be;
He zwore he zid bold Renyard
    Run up a hollow tree."—*Old Hunting Song.*

RESOLUTE. Strong, hardy.

"'Twull be a job to tackle'n, vor he's a gurt resolute feller, you know."

RETCH *(A.S. ræcan).* To stretch, to try to vomit.

RICE. A long, supple branch of underwood.

"If thee doesn't mind what thee bist up to, bwoy, thee'st git the rice."

(Two girls going home together):—"Oh! I zay, Polly, han't ye ben and tore a gurt slit in your frock!" "Have I? Oh my, shan't I ketch it when I gits hooam! Mother'll prid near skin me, and make a night cap wi' the peel." *(They part, and Polly arrives home)*:—"Wher'st thee ben too, Poll? I ben waaiten vor a nower vor ye to goo and git me zome milk; and I've a very good mind to gee thee a good basten. But how ded ye tear yer frock like that, ye young faggot? Thee'st ben in copse agen, picken kettle caps and oxslips. I'll git a rice, and rice thee down till thee doesn't know where thee bist on thee head or thee heels; and not one bit o' supper thee shatunt hay. Goo 'long upstairs to bed, ye good-for-nothen young huzzy; I'll let thee know when I comes up there predney." *(The two girls meeting again next day)*:—"How ded ye git on last night about yer frock, Polly?" "Oh, mother packed me off to bed wi'out ar supper, and then she come up wi' a rice, and pulled me out o' bed; and dedn't she twank me! I never had sich a ricen avore, and dedn't I roar and squall! they could hear me round the carner."

RICK. A sprain.
"I've bin and ricked my yarm now."—I have sprained my arm.

RICKESS. A rick yard.
"We must plaay in, mayet, if all this corn es to be got into rickess avore nammet time."

RID. Red.
"There's zome colour vor ye, mayet." "Oi you, 'tes blood rid all over, like varmer Trell's waggon."

RIDDLE. Ruddle, a composition of red ochre, used to mark sheep.

RIDE. To get angry when teased or bantered.
"We got on to Tom about the wold mallard, and dedn't he ride and zwear over it."

RIDGIONER. A horse half castrated.

RIDGTY. A chain passing over the horse's back, to support the shafts of a cart or waggon.

RIDWEED. The poppy, *Papaver rhœas*.

RIG. To climb, or play in wantonness, to break through a fence.
"Zet down, I tell'ee! you'll tear yer clothes all to pieces, a riggen about zo."

RIGGISH. Applied to sheep or cattle breaking through fences and getting out of a field.

"That's a terbul riggish heifer o' your'n, varmer; she's for ever gitten' over hedge into my vatches."

RIG OUT. To hoax, or bamboozle; to cram with a fictitious story.

"I minds one time I was in the 'Hare an Houns' at Downend, you, and who should come in but wold Jolliffe, that used to live over at Waaitshill, or Stooanshill, zomewhere out about Buttbridge, and a had his yarm in a sling. 'Hollo meyaster!' zomebody zays too'n, 'what have ye hurt your hand?' 'Iss,' a zays, 'I have. T'other day I was tryen to git down a gurt kite bough, and a broke off wi' me, and I vell out o' the tree and broke me yarm, and it harls me up miserable, now jest grass cutten time, too.' 'Well, 'tes a bad job vor ye,' zays a chap zetten 'long zide on 'en, that worked in the marl pit handy the house; 'but if you'll stand half-a-gallon o' beer, I can gee ye a resayt that'll keep ye vrom ever vallen out of a tree any more zo long as ye be alive.' I could zee he was gwyne to rig the wold man out, you know you. 'Well,' zays wold Jolliffe, 'I *should* like to hay that; 'tes fair doos, I spooase.' 'Oi you,' zays t'other, ''tis right enough if ye onny goos by't.' Zo the wold man orders in the beer, and when 'twas about all drinked he zays, 'Now then, let's hay this resayt ye promised me.' 'All right, wold bwoy,' zays the chap, 'here 'tes; and if ye always volleys it you'll never vall out o' or tree any more, I'll be bound. Don't tich noo kite boughs ye can't raych standen on yer ligs, and ye'll never break any of yer booans nor vall down, let it be how 'twull.' Dedn't the wold man rare at 'en! he got zo mad, a could hardly spake. 'If 'twuddent vor my yarm,' a zed, 'ye hang-gallus rogue, I'd lance thee jacket well vor thee.' But we all bust out in a reglar haw, haw, and a jumped up and off a went in a terbul pelt."

RIMEY. Hazy, slightly foggy.

RINE. Rind, the bark of a tree; also, skin.

"I het my lig agen that skote jest now, and I zee it took a bit o' the rine off."

RINE OFF. To strip.

"Wold Dick talked about rinen off and clouten on 'en."

RIP. To reap; also, a worthless person. When applied to a female,—vile, unchaste.

"He's a reglar wold rip; don't hay nothen to do wi' 'en."

RIPHOOK. A reaping hook, a sickle.

Rish. To rush. "Rish to cut," or "Rish to leather."—To ride or drive fast, or at a great rate.

"I was worken down Crannidge's one time, hedgen and deetchen, you; and all at once I heerd zummet hissen and snoppen like a bag o' warnuts gwyne rish droo copse. Zo I goos to zee what was up, and I comes across a bobby's nest vull o' gurt big young ones, and there was mister scorpian (a snake) jest gwyne to scoff 'em up. I up wi' my stakebittle and let drave down across 'en, and a went down droo the cath zomewhere, vor I never zid no more on 'en aaterwards."

Roke (reek). Steam from boiling water, slaked lime, or from a newly made rick.

"Putt on the pot led: look how the roke vlees out all over the place." "The haayrick rokes a good deal moore than I likes."

Rongs. The rungs or steps of a ladder.

Ronk. Growing strong or luxuriantly; also, strong tasted or smelling.

Rot gut. Small beer.

"Hurrah, varmer Ben! how bist? Thee doesn't look very pert jest at present." "Noa, I don't spooase I do, vor I don't veel over toppen, and kindy queer in my innerds, I can tell'ee. I yet zome apple pudden at dinnertime, and then I went down to wold Beagle's, and was fool enough to git a pint or two of his rot gut into me, and 'tes sarren me out cruel. I shan't doo't agen, I'll war nt it."

Rough. Ill, or sick.

"How be ye gitten on, you? ye ben led up, han't ye?" "Iss, I have; but I be gitten round agen now; I was terbul rough vor a bit."

Rowet. Coarse, rough grass, growing generally among furze or brushwood.

Rowse. To disturb, to drive or put out.

"Goo and rowse they there fowls out o' gearden."

Roxell. To wrestle.

Rudder (*A.S. hrudrian*, to sift). A sieve; also, to shake one's head.

"I've heerd my father tell o' wold Forred, what used to be clark at Newchurch, and played a hobwoy in church a Zundays; another wold feller, that lived at Pigspond, used to plaay a bazoon or zummet o' the sort there besides. One Zunday, aater the sarmon, they had to zing the Wold Hundred; but when the paason—Gill, I thinks hes naame was—finished up, wold Forred was vast asleep. 'Tother wold man nudges 'en, and zays, 'Come, come, Richard, let's strick up.' 'All right!' zings out wold Forred, about half awake, 'I'll lay two half-crowns on the rid cock.' The paason ruddered hes head at 'en when a heerd it; but a dedn't zay nothen too'n, as I knows on."

RUE. A small strip of coppice.

RUE IN. In haymaking, to put two or three swathes into one.
"Look sharp and finish ruein in that haay, and let's begin pooken."

RUM. Eccentric, odd.
"He's a miserable rum wold feller."

RUN. To grow; also, to have an outlet or demand for.
"These turmets be all run to zeed." "He got sich a good run for his barley, always."

RUN DOWN. To depreciate, to speak disparagingly of.

RUSTY. Restive; angry, or morose.
"The wold dooman sims terbul rusty over it."

S.

SAACY. Pert, insolent; also, wanton or skittish.
"Don't you be zo saacy, bwoy, or I shall clout yer years."
"That hoss was turned out in the meead, 'till he got zo saacy we had to take 'en in and putt'n to plough."

SAAVEALL. An appendage to a candlestick or lantern, to burn the candle ends.

SAFE. Sure, or certain.
"He's safe to be there Zadderday."

SAMPER. Samphire.

SAR. To serve, to feed animals.
"That jest sar'd 'en right.'
"I thinks about gwyne to Nippert predney; d'ye want anything? And I was gwyne to ax ye if ye wouldn't mind sarren my pig at dinner-time; I've mixed the vittles up all ready vor'n." "All right, I'll sar'n vor ye; and I sholl be glad if ye'll goo into Daycon's and git me half-a-yard o Rooshian card, to mend my wold man's breeches wi'.'

SCALE. To throw stones, to pelt anything.

"They bwoys be out there scalen the apple trees: I sholl be aater 'em wi' a stick." "That chap scaled the pigs all down the road."

SCALEY. Mean, shabby, or stingy.

"He's a miserable scaley sort o' feller: you'll git nothen out on 'en vor your trouble."

SCOAT. A prop or shore, generally used for a rick.

"Come on, mayet, we must goo and scoat up that wheeat rick, else he'll be all about house avore mornen."

SCOFF. To eat, to devour.

"I axed 'em to hay a mouthful o' vittles, and they zet down and scoffed every bit o' grub there was on the taable: they dedn't leave a mite o' nothen for noobody else, but scoggelled up the lot."

SCOGGEL. To eat voraciously; to gulp or swallow anything without chewing it.

SCOOP. A broad wooden or iron shovel. Those used in barns are made of wood, and are called "barn scoops."

SCOTCH. To cut or notch anything.

SCRAALD. Corn, when nearly ready for harvest, blown about in different directions.

SCRAN BAG. A bag in which a labourer carries his dinner; called, also, "dinner bag."

SCRANNEL. To eat greedily, to gobble up.

SCRAZE. To graze.

"I've scrazed my elbow a bit."

SCREECH OWL. The bull thrush.

"There used to be dree or vour wold women about here one time, who used to prid near frighten all the vokes in the parish out o' what little sense they had. There was wold granny Jooans, and wold granny Morris, and one or two more wold brimstooane bitches, that was vor ever zeein' tokens, and ghoates, and signs, and noobody knows what nonsense bezides; and a gurt many people was zoat enough to bleeve sich traade, and used to goo to 'em vor charms, and to hay their fortunes toold. One day vour or vive was got together in granny zomebody's house—I vorgits which 'twas now—but howsomever there was a larkish kind o' chap handy, that zid the lot goo in,—I thinks his naame was Jacobs,—zo he thought he'd jest like to hear what they was on upon; zo he slips over hedge into the gearden, and crapes in under the open winder. There they was round the taable, tellen fortunes in their teacups: one was to hay a carriage stop at her door, and another was to zee a strainger avore night, and a lot moore o' sich wold zoat foolishness; and then one on 'em begun to tell how she heerd a screech owl several times the night avore, and 'twas a sartain token o' death to zomebody or nother she knowed. 'Iss,' zays another, 'one vlow cloose by my uncle's head, and gid a terbul screech, and the poor wold man come hooam and went to bed, and was a corpse avore the week was out.' Then another wold fool toold a yarn about a gurt high thing all in white, that she zid one mornen in wold Cooper's gearden, avore 'twas light, when she was gwyne out to washen. 'Ah!' zays the wold dooman the house belonged to, 'ouny last night I was putten a vew sticks under my kettle to bwoil'n up vor my tay, when all at once the room simmed to git mummy; zo I looked up, and massy me! if there wudden't a gurt ugly black thing, wi' eyes ver' near as big as the top o' one o' these taycups, jest outside the winder, staren in at me: I ded gee sich a squawk.' While all this was gwyne on, Jacobs whipped down the gearden and got a wold gallybagger that was there, and ties 'en on to the wold dooman's oben rubber that was layen agen the wall, and direckly minute the wold fool was tellen how she squawked at the gurt black thing she zid the night avore, Jacobs rammed the wold gallybagger right droo winder, on top o' the taable, right in the middle on 'em. They dedn't stop to hay a second look at it, but roared out, and vlow out o' doors like bees out o' a tee hole. 'Twas zome time avore they come back, and while they was away Jacobs putt the gallybagger in his plaace agen; zo they dedn't know the geeam he had wi' 'em. But the yoppel they maade over it terrified their neighbours zo, that lots on 'em was afeared to goo out doors in the dark vor months aaterwards."

SCRILE. Underwood, brushwood.

SCRIM. To grasp forcibly, so as to bruise or crush anything.
"He's ben and scrimmed the letter up."

SCRIMPY. Small, or mean.
"Well, that es a scrimpy bit o' pork."

SCROFF. Dead wood fallen under trees; also, refuse of faggots or straw.
"I can't het the oben, vor I got nothen to keep the vire up wi' but a lot o' wold scroff."

SCROOP. To creak, or grate; as a pair of new shoes, a cartwheel wanting grease, or the rusty hinges of a door.

"I can hear that keert-wheel scroop half-a-mile off; a must be graced when we gits into rickess." "I got a pair o' new shoes on, and they *do scroop*, I can tell'ee."

SCROW. Cross-looking, of ill appearance, scowling.

SCRUMP. Baked hard; short in eating.

"These biscuits yet nice and scrump, you, wi' a bit o' cheese."

SCRUNCH. To crunch, or crush with an audible sound.

"That dog *es* scrunchen the booans up."

SCRUNGE. To squeeze or press.

"Don't keep on scrungen me up in the corner zo."

SCUD. A slight, or passing, shower.

"How bist this mornen, you? Gwyne to git zome raain, d'ye think?" "Well, I dunno what to make on't. I zee the wind's draawed away in round clooser; but it med be onny a bit o' a scud aater all."

SCUDDICK. A morsel; sometimes, a small coin.

"There edden't a scuddick on't left." "I can't lend ye tuppence, vor I hain't got a scuddick about me."

SCUFF *(A.S. scúfan).* To scrape the feet on the ground in walking; to walk in a slipshod manner.

"Why doesn't lift thee ligs off the ground? thee'st very zoon scuff the zoles o' thee boots out else."

SETTLE. The foundation, of timber, faggots, &c. (generally raised on stone pillars), of a rick; a long high-backed seat, used in kitchens.

SHAB OFF. To sneak or shuffle off.

"I zay, Bob, hast thee zid our keerter's mayet about here anywhere?" "Oi you, he was here, zetten on the barn door rack, while I was keaven up jest now; but when I looked round agen, a was shabbed off."

SHACKLES. Twisted slips of hazel or willow, in the shape of a ring, to fasten hurdles to stakes or posts.

SHAKES. "He's noo gurt shakes."—He is no great things, or nothing to boast of.

SHARP. To sharpen.

"Wull'ee lend me your whetstooan, you? I wants to sharp my riphook."

SHAT. Shall. "Shatn't."—Shall not.
"Thee shatn't goo down shore to-day, let it be how 'twull.'
—You shall not go down to the shore to-day, let whatever will happen, or be the consequences of it.

SHELTEN IN. The shortening of the days; the dusk or twilight.
"Aater Michaelmas the days begin shelten in vast."

SHET. To weld together, as two pieces of iron.

SHET OFF. To unyoke horses from the plough; to end the day's work with horses.
"What time d'ye think 'tes, mayet?" "I dunno, you; but vrom the look o' the zun, I louz 'tes prid near shet off time."

SHICKSHACK. Oak leaves and apples, worn on Royal Oak day, in memory of Charles II.,—principally by boys, and now almost obsolete. The juveniles, with their hats and caps bedecked with oak leaves, went about repeating the following couplet:—
"The twenty-ninth o' May
Es shickshack day,"
—till noon, when the commemoration was supposed to be ended.

SHIM. A flitting shadow.
"Now I can't zackly zay if he's gone hooam or no; but I louz a med be, vor I jest ketched the shim o' zomebody gwyne past the door jest now."—I can't exactly say if he is gone home or not; but I think he might be, for I caught a glimpse of the shadow of someone going past the door just now.

SHIRK. To slink or sneak off; to evade in a sly or cowardly manner.
"He's ben and shirked off wi'out dooen his work." "He's too windy by half, and he's sure to shirk out on't zomehow or nother."—He's too wheedling, or plausible, and is sure to evade or sneak out of his obligations in some way.

SHIRT OUT. To get anyone's "shirt out," or make him "shirty," is to make him get into a passion, or very angry, by teasing, bantering, or jeering him,—to the delight of his tormentors.
"I zid wold Mussell gwyne by yesterday, you, and I zung out too'n, 'Hast pinned ar a pig's innerds layetly?' and dedn't he jest about get shirty! Hes shirt was out direckly, and a talked about rinen off vor me; zo I slipped along and left 'en zwaaren in the road."

SHOOT. A steep hill in a road or lane; also, a young growing pig.

"He ver' near auverdrode the dungpot gwyne down Newchurch Shoot." "I shan't be gwyne out o' town jest dircckly, you; vor I must goo into market and zee if I can't buy a couple of shoots."

SHOW HACKLE. To get ready, or be willing, to fight. An expression derived from a cock erecting his "hackles," or feathers about his neck, before beginning to fight.

"One Whitsuntide, a good many years ago now you, I was in Johnny Buckler's out at Caaburn, and 'long come one o' the Jackmans vrom Brison, a terbul maggoty kind o' feller, you know you. A brought in zummet in a bag wi' 'en, and simm'd mortal keerful over't; zo zomebody axed, 'What hav'ee got there, you?' and a zays, 'What have I got? why, zomethen nobody in the Island ever zid avore—a churry-coloured cat, mayet.' 'Let's hay a look at he, then,' zed several at once. 'Noa,' zays Jackman, 'that won't do it [yet], I must hay a handsel avore the bag's opened; 'tes wuth drippence apiece to zee sich a out and out cat as this es; but as 'tes Fair-time and all, you sholl zee the cat vor a penny apiece, jest vor once.' Zo they chucked a penny all round into Jackman's hat, and he claaed it out and putt it into hes pocket, and dedn't sim in a hurry to untie the bag. Zo one or two zays too'n, 'Now then, mayet, look sharp and open the zack, and stoor out this churry-colour cat;' and a opened the bag, and out jumped a gurt black cat, wi' eyes like rid hot coals, and vlow out o' winder and across the road like a shot. Zome on 'em dedn't half like it, and got shirty about it, and begun to show hackle and talk about clouten on 'en; but Jackman maade us all laugh, for a zed, 'Look here now, chaps, 'tes all square enough, vor there's black churries, edden't there, as well as rid ones; and that cat's black enough vor anybody, I'll war'nt it.' Zo he ordered in half-a-gallon wi' the money he'd got, and it all passed off very well."

SHOW OFF. To scold or rate, to reprimand; also, to go through a performance.

"I let the cows get into the clover, and dedn't meyaster show off at me about it!" "When be the Moll Andrey's gwyne to show off, mayet?" "Oh, I heerd one o' the show fellers zay 'twould be about dree o'clock in the aaternoon, you."

SHOW TO. To accept a challenge to fight; to undertake anything.

"It s no use vor he to show to wold Harry; he's too good a

F

man vor'n."—It's no use for him to attempt to fight old Harry, &c. "I sims kindy rough this mornen, you; I can't show to noo vittles."—I feel out of sorts this morning, and have no appetite for food.

SHRAMMED.   Benumbed, or shrunk up with cold.
"Let's get avore the vire and hay a bit of a het, vor I be ver' near shrammed; my vingers be like ice."

SHRIP. To cut or whittle away a piece of wood, to make chips, to clip a hedge.

SHROKE.   Shrivelled.
"They there apples be all shroke up to nothen."

SHROVEN. Children going from house to house and singing for cakes, on Shrove Tuesday. The children were called "Shrovers," and the cakes given them "Shrove cakes." This old custom, like most others, has now fallen into desuetude; but about forty years ago the children of a parish or neighbourhood assembled early in the morning of Shrove Tuesday, and visited the houses of the principal inhabitants in succession, beginning with the gentry and ending with the farmers. If the supply of cakes ran short, pence, bread and cheese, or pancakes were substituted; and in very few cases indeed were the "Shrovers" sent away empty. A song, used only on these occasions, was sung, and those who sang it the loudest were considered the best "Shrovers," and often got an extra cake or penny in consequence. The song varied a little in different parts of the Island, but generally ran as follows:—

"Shroven, Shroven,
I be come a Shroven.
A piece of bread, a piece of cheese,
A piece of your fat baacon,
Doughnuts and pancakes,
All o' your own maaken;
Vine vowls in a pie,
My mouth es very dry,
I wish I was zo well a-wet,
I'd zing the better vor a nut.
Shroven, Shroven,
We be come a Shroven."

SHROVY, or SHREAVY. Poor, applied to land; want of depth of soil.

SHUCKS. The husks or shells of peas or beans, after the seeds have been taken out.

SIGHT. A large quantity, a number.

"There was a sight o' people at varmer Way's zale, you."

SIM. To seem; also, to feel.

"I sims terbul kind o' sleepy this aaternoon, mayet."

SIMMEN. Seeming, appearing.

"Simmen to me you'd better let that job alooan."—It seems to me—or, in my opinion—you had better not do so-and-so.

SIMPLE. Weak minded, foolish, semi-idiotic.

"He es that simple, he takes in everything that's toold 'en."

SINGREEN *(A.S. sın-gréne).* The house leek, *semper vivum tectorum.* Its leaves are considered to be cooling, and, mixed with cream, are used to cure eruptions.

SITHE. To sigh or sob.

SKEEAS. Scarce, uncommon.

SKEEATHY, or SCATHY. Thievish, sneaking.

"Have ye got ar a dog to gee away, varmer? I had to putt a charge o' shot into my wold dog last week; he was got zo skeeathy, there was noo keepen nothen out o' the jaas on 'en. I had a duck zetten in the keert house, and a yet up all the iggs, and zwalleyed the wold duck aaterwards; vor all I could vind on her was a bit of a wing and a vew veathers layen about."

SKENT. The diarrhœa, or looseness of the bowels, in cattle.

"That 'ere heifer o' your'n es a '*skenter*'"—*i.e.*, an animal that will not fatten.

SKICE. To frisk or race about, to frolic.

"Don't the mice skice round house in the night, you!"

SKILLEN. The back part of a cottage or farm house; a penthouse.

SKITTER-BOOT. A heavy, hobnailed boot, worn by labourers.

SKIVER. A skewer.

SKIVER WOOD. The wood of which skewers are generally made,—Spindle tree, *euonymus Europœus.*

SLAABACK. A great clumsy, or ignorant, person.

"Hast zid the fresh maade at varmer White's it, you? She *es* a gurt slaabacked thing, from what I can zee on her."—Have you seen the new maid at farmer White's yet? She *is* a great clumsy person, from what I can see of her.

SLACK. Impertinence or abuse; also, to be indolent.

"Don't let's hay noo moore o' yer slack here, or out doors ye goos neck and crop, sharp."—Let us have no more of your impertinence, or you will be thrown out of doors at once. "That bwoy sims mortal slack to-day."—That boy seems very indolent to-day.

SLACKUMTRANCE. A slovenly or dirty woman.

"I never thought much on her: she always was a gurt slackumtrance thing, to my mind."

SLAMMAKIN. Untidy, careless, slovenly.

"I won't hay things done in sich a slammaken way: 'twun't do vor me."

SLAP UP. To be slap up, is to be quite well, to look well, or to be well dressed.

"Hows't git on, you?" "Oh, slap up, mayet." "I zid Jack Zunday evenen, and a was looken slap up,—better than ever I zid 'en avore."

SLAT. To strike or slap; to throw down, or to throw water about.

"If thee doesn't gee off roaren, I'll slat thee." "He brought the things in, and slat 'em down bout house."

SLETCH. To stop or cease; also, to slake lime.

"We cut and keerted twenty acres one year, you, in dree days; but I don't want another sich a job; 'twas hard slaavery and noo sletch in it, vrom mornen to night."

SLIM. Slight, or slender.

"He's growen up a tallish, slim chap, now."

SLINK. A small piece of wet meadow land; also, a weak or half-starved animal.

"That heifer *es* a slink of a thing."

SLIPS. Young growing pigs.

SLOUCH. To walk in a shambling manner; to slink about.

"There goos wold Jem Stretch, slouchen along, wi' hes rags vleein' in the wind."

SLUED. Intoxicated, drunk.

"He ben to Cowes wi' a looad o' barley, and come back about dree parts slued; as much as ever he can zee a hole in a ladder."

SLUGGARD'S GUISE. A sluggard's manner, or sluggardly habit; hence the rhyme applied to lazy children:—

"Thee bist sluggard's guise,
Loth to goo to bed, and loth to rise."

SLUSH. Wet mud.

"Here's our Hen wi' hes new clothes on, and a must needs git riggen up top o' the pig's house and vall down into the slush, and a pretty pickle he's in. I'll take the rine off the back on un when I gits 'en indoors."—Here's our Henry with his new clothes on, and he must go and climb up on the pig's house and fall down into the wet mud—or filth. A pretty mess he's in. I'll take the skin off his back when he comes indoors.

SLUTTISH. Dirty or drizzling weather.

"Hollo, missus! how be ye? Terrábble sluttish to-day, edden't it?"

SMAAM. To smear or daub with paint or tar.

"Have ye zid the wold cappender about here layetly?" "A was here yesterday, smaamen over the barn's door wi' a tar brish, but I han't zid nothen on 'en zunce."

SMELLERS. The whisker hairs of a cat.

SMIRT. Quick, adroit, smart; also, quantity, or distance.

"There's a smirt lot on't left it."—There's a good deal of it left yet.

SMOCKFAACED. Bashful, beardless, sheepish.

SMOCK FROCK. A labourer's white round frock.

SNAAIL'S TROT. Walking very slowly; crawling along.

SNAAKE'S-STANG. The Dragon-fly. These insects are often found in the Island of a larger size than usual, and very brilliant in colour. They are popularly supposed to have a sting which is as venomous as the bite of a viper or an adder, and are dreaded accordingly. Being generally to be seen in the vicinity of brooks and ponds, they were also considered to be the guardians of the fish, and to sting all improper persons who attempted to catch them. Children held them in great fear, and on the appearance of a

"Snake's-stang," used to sing or repeat the following rhyme as a kind of charm or protection against the noxious insect:—

"Snake's-stang, Snake's-stang, vlee all about the brooks,
And sting all the bad bwoys that vor the fishes looks;
But let all the good bwoys ketch all the fish they can,
And car 'em away hooam to fry 'em in the pan.
Bren butter they sholl yet at supper wi' their fish,
But all the little bad bwoys sholl onny lick the dish."

How the "Snake's-stang" could distinguish between the good and bad "bwoys" is altogether inexplicable.

SNARKER. A word of very little definite meaning, but used thus:—

"The cake's burnt to a snarker"—*i.e.*, burnt up—or to a cinder.

SNAWF. The snuff of a candle; also, to trim or cut off the tapering roots of turnips or carrots.

"I be gwyne snawffen turmets to-morrow, you."

SNEEAD. The pole or handle of a scythe.

"I must goo down to blacksmith's shop to-night, and git a new ring vor my zive sneead."

SNOACH. To snuffle, to speak through the nose.

"I zay you, d'ye mind that 'ere Smith, that went by the naame o' 'Skaymer'? A used to hay a miserable snoach wi' 'en, and lived at Caaburn Bottom one time,—the plaace you know, you, where they makes Olmanecks, and putts in the rid letters down in the bottom of the well. One day Skaymer was out our way about zummet or nother, and was talken to mey-aster and the bwoy (he's growed up now), and a zays, 'What be ye gwyne to make o' your bwoy here, meyaster?' 'Well,' meyaster zed, 'I can't hardly tell it; but mooast likely I sholl make a buttcher on 'en.' 'If that's what ye meeans to do wi' 'en,' zays Skaymer, 'you'd better putt'n wi' wold Doctor Clarke down at Yarmouth, vor he's the biggest buttcher I ever zid, or heerd on in this country.'"

SNOBBLE. To devour greedily, to snap up,—as ducks eating slugs.

SNOOZLE (sometimes SNOODLE). To nestle, to lie close together; also, to rub and scratch, and attend assiduously to pigs.

"I zee the wold zow and the pigs be all snoozled in together."

In a case of pig-stealing tried many years ago at Winchester, the chief witness for the prosecution was asked by the opposing counsel why he was so positive in swearing to the stolen pigs, as all pigs were very much alike. "Why," said the witness, "I'll tell'ee vor why: cause *I snoodled 'em*, and could prid near undertake to zware to every heer on their backs." The term "*snoodled 'em*" was a poser to counsel and judge, and an explanation was called for; when it was found to mean that the witness had attended to the pigs daily, feeding them constantly with different things, and in rubbing and scratching their backs had employed all his leisure time.

SNOP. A sharp or quick blow.

"The wold dooman was roasten some taeties under the grate—they *ded* smill good,—and I tried to claa out one or two; but I wudden't quite smirt enough, vor she gid me sich a snop on the vingers wi' the short-handled brish, that they ached vor half an hour."

SOGGED. Saturated with wet.

SOLID. Serious, or grave looking.

"He dedn't zay nothen, but he looked terbul solid about it."

SOMEWHEN. At some time or other.

SOWL. To pull the ears of a person; or, a dog fastening on the ears of an animal.

"The dog gid the wold zow a middlen sowlen all round the ground, avore she got to the gap."

SOWSE. The ears, feet, and tail of a pig, pickled and boiled.

"The taailor he shot, but he missed hes mark,
And he shot hes wold zow right droo and droo her heart.

. . . .

'Od dang it!' zays the taailor, 'I don't keer a louse,
Vor I sholl hay black puddens, chitlens, and sowse.'"
—*Old Song.*

SPARS. Sticks of hazel or withy,—split, pointed, twisted, and doubled in the middle,—used to fasten the thatch to ricks and houses.

SPARK-ED *(A.S. spearca).* Speckled or spotted.

SPAT. A blow with the flat of the hand, a slight slap. "Spats."—Short leggings. "Breeches and spats" were the height of fashion with the "Bucks" of the Island sixty years ago.

SPEARS. The hands of a clock or watch; also, the shoots of potatoes when stored in a heap.

"The spears o' my watch be got harled up zomehow; they won't goo round."—The hands of my watch are entangled in some manner; they won't go round. "I sholl be at hooam all day to-day, vor we be gwyne to spear our taeties"—*i.e.*, to break the shoots off the potatoes to preserve them.

SPELL. A short time, an interval; also, to insinuate, to ask indirectly.

"Take hold o' the rake and gee us a bit of a spell, wull'ee you"—*i.e.* an interval of rest. "That wold feller wants me to lend 'en my puncheon now 'tes harvest time. He ben here spellen vor'n a time or two; but a edden't gwyne to hay'n, vor I sholl want to use 'en myself."

SPILE. A wooden vent peg for a cask.

SPIRES. A coarse kind of rushes; the stems of the *carex paniculata*, or similar sedges.

SPIT-DEEP. The depth of earth turned up by a spade when digging.

SPLAA. Broad, ill made.

"That Will Reynolds *es* a gurt, unhandy, lop-yeared looken feller, and the gurt splaa veet on 'en es about the size o' zeedlips. Wold Jeans, the shoemaker, used to zay hes shop wudden't big enough to make boots vor Reynolds in—he hadn't got room there to turn 'em round, zo he was fooaced to goo out into geearden and make 'em under a tree."

SPREADER. The piece of wood, or bar, between the chain traces of the horses in a team.

SPUDGEL. A small bucket, with a long stick for a handle, used for bailing out water.

"Hollo mayet! thee looks as if thee'st ben droo hedge backards. What's up wi' thee?" "Oh! my back's ver' near broke. I come across a hin's nest under a settle last night, you, wi' zix iggs in 'en. I zucked vive, and was jest agwyne to git rid o' t'other, when wold 'Billygoat" come round the corner o' the barn and ketched me, and, wuss luck, there was a spudgel up agen the barn's door, zo the wold man vlow in and claaed hold by the spudgel, and smeared in athurt my back wi' booath hands, and knocked me down as flat as a pancake; I thought my back was broke vor a minute or two. 'There Tom,' a zed to me, 'that'll spwile thy appetite for any moore o' my iggs,' and zo it ded; I dedn't zwalley the last on 'em, but slipped off as sharp as I could."

SPURRETS. Spirits; gin, rum, or brandy.

SQUASH. To crush, to bruise.

SQUAWK. To squall or squeak.

"I haates to hear a lot o' young ones squawken when I be indoors."

SQUAWKEN THRUSH. The missel thrush.

SQUEAL. To squeak.

"She squealed like a wold zow hung up in a hurdle."

SQUENCH. To quench.

SQUINNY. To fret or cry as a child; also, lean or thin.

"What a squinny little bit of a pig!"

SQUINNY GUTS. A fretful or peevish child.

"That maade o' your'n es a regler squinny guts. If she belonged to me, I believe I should knock the head on her off."

SQUISH. To squeeze or gush out.

"I was gwyne down the layen in the dark, and all at once I went right over boots in the keert loose; zoo the water squished out o' my boots as I walked."

SQUITTERS (sometimes SQUIRTS). The diarrhœa or looseness in cattle.

SQUOT. To sit on the ground; also, to bruise or dint anything by a blow.

"I'm prid near fagged out, zo I sholl jest squot down under hedge here vor vive minutes."

STAABIT. A mouthful or two of food taken between meals, a staybit; generally, a piece of bread and cheese before dinner.

STABBLE. To walk about on and soil a newly cleaned floor with wet or dirty boots.

"If missus comes in, won't she show off at thee vor maken all that stabble bout house! Thee'st git it!"

STALL. A partition in a stable; also, a covering or case for a sore finger.

"I got a gatheren comen on my vinger: wull'ee make me a stall vor'n, missus, playse."

STAFF HOOK. A reaping hook or sickle with a long handle, used to cut pease and trim hedges.

STALE. Slow, sluggish.
"That bwoy sims terbul stale to-day: I sholl stoor'n up wi' the whip predney."

STAND TO. To insist on or substantiate anything; also, to be sponsor to a child.

STANDVURDER. A contention, a quarrel.
"Wold Jerry Bull ben dead now a good many years; I can onny jest mind 'en. A used to be a kind o' groom or coachman to Squire Rishwuth [Rushworth], who lived at Freshwater one time. The Squire couldn't bear turnpike geats—they was jest putt up then; a wouldn't never paay if a could help it, and always had a deuce of a standvurder wi' the turnpike feller. 'Drave rish droo,' he'd zay to Jerry, 'I'll stand the racket on't.' One day, the Squire was took mortal bad, and thought a was gwyne off the hooks; zo a had wold Jerry in to zay good-bye too'n. 'Ah Jerry,' a zed, 'I be gwyne a longer journey now than ever you drove me.' 'Well, meyaster,' zays Jerry, 'ye won't hay to paay noo turnpikes on the road, that'll be one consolation to ye.'"

START. An upshot, a fuss, a disturbance.
"Here's a middlen start, you! Our keerter's ben and 'listed for a sojer."

STAST. To stop, to give up, to abandon; also, to flag.

STEAN. To line or lay with stones. (Now almost obsolete.)
"We found aftor ye inninge of ye Haven [Brading], almost in ye middle thereof, a well steined with stones, which argueth it had binn firme lande and inhabited."—*Sir J. Oglander's MS.*

STERRUP. A leather band used by shoemakers to hold a boot in its place while being sewn.

STERRUP ILE. Unsuspecting or dull youths were often sent by their seniors to the village cobbler with a request for "Sterrup ile," to quicken their apprehension; but which the petitioners found to their cost, consisted in a vigorous application of the *sterrup* to their shoulders; the cobbler always thinking it his duty to give as good measure as possible of his oil when asked for it, especially as he was certain the recipient would never come again for more.

"When I was a gurt hard bwoy, one time, out in the rickess at Wroxall wi' that 'ere maggotty Sam Jacobs, a zed to me: 'Goo down to cobbler Coombes's vor me, wull'ee, and ax 'en to gee ye a drap o' hes best sterrup ile; there's noo call vor ye to take anything to car et in.' Zo, like a fool, off I goos, and axed the wold man vor't. A was zet there, zowen away; but as zoon as I toold'n what I was come vor, a rared up and took hes sterrup off his knee, and draaed en dree or vower times right across my showlders, ready to cut me all to pieces. 'There's the ile,' a zays, 'and I've rubbed it in vor thee.' I roared out, and shabbed off as quick as I could, looken middlen foolish; and I've always minded what *sterrup ile* was vrom that day to this."

STEW. Anxiety, misgiving, or fear.
"I dedn't know how 'twould turn out, and I was in a terbul stew about it tell 'twas all over."

STICK. A tree.
"That's a fine stick o' tember."—That's a fine timber tree.

STILLURS. Steelyards, for weighing.

STITCH. A rood of land; also, a pain in the side after running.

STIVER UP. To bristle or brush up, as hair.
"Hes heear was stivered up middlen."

STOCKY. Stout, thick-set.
"He's got a short, stocky chap, now."

STOOAN. A stone. "Stooan hoss."—A stallion.

STOOR. To stir a liquid; also, to turn or drive out.

STOP-GAP. A substitute, one put in from necessity, to fill the place of a better man for a time.
"I bean't a gwyne to be maade a stop-gap on vor noobody, if I knows it."

STOUT *(A.S. stút)*. A fly that stings cattle; the gad-fly.
"My eyes, you! the heifers got the stout, and be all gone taail-on-end, right down droo the clover, and rish droo hedge into copse."

STRAAIN. To strain; also, a farrow or litter of pigs.
"My zow got a fine straain o' ten pigs this mornen."

STRAA-VORK. A large wooden fork, shaped like the letter Y, used to carry straw for thatching stacks or houses. A long-legged person, of either sex, is often nicknamed "Straa-vorks."

STRADDLE. To stride; to stand or move with the legs wide apart. A woman riding a horse like a man is said to ride "*astraddle.*"

STRAKE. One piece of the iron used to "*bond*" a wheel.

STRETCH. A piece of straight wood used to sweep over the top of the bushel when filled,—a strike.

STRICK. To strike. " Strick in here."—Begin working just in this spot or place.

STROGS. Short leather gaiters, very similar to "Spats," *(which see)*.

STROKERS. The last milk drawn from a cow in milking.

STUBBERDS. A variety of the apple.

STUFFLE. To stifle.

"I jest ben up top o' the haayrick, and a's hetten zoo, the roke ver' near stuffled me: a was putt together too quick."

STURTLE. To frighten, to startle.

"Hollo you! deds't get woke up last night?" " I'll war'nt it, mayet; gullies, dedn't it blow and thunder and lighten! I was afeared to lay in bed, zo I turned out, vor I was regler sturtled like." " But where be you off to this way?" " Why, down shore you: a ship come in last night." " Ded there? then here's off long wi' ye; noo doubt we sholl pick up zummet or nother, mayet. Dost know what she's loaded wi'?" " Oh, pineapples and oranges; or somethen like it,—zoo Will Buckett toold me. The life-boat went out to 'em, and saaved thirteen; but vower on 'em got drownded." " You don't zay zoo! Well, the zooner we gits down shore the better, then."

SUANT. Smooth, even, regular, equally distributed.

"That's a suant piece of barley you got in Barnclose, varmer." " My keerter toold me he knowed how to zow a vew acres; but he don't sim to do it at all suant, to my mind."

SURGE. A quick motion, force, or collision.

"I was out in gearden, hoen tacties, when I zees the hoss and trap comen down the road stretch gallop; and they come wi' sich a surge up agen the corner o' the wall, that it knocked one o' the wheels clean off, and auverdrowed the hoss and all."

SWAAILEN. Walking in a rolling and lazy manner.

"Here comes wold Bung Russel, swaailen along as if a was gwyne to vall to pieces. He ought to be maade chaairman o' the Laazy Club."

SWEAL *(A.S. swélan).* To singe or scorch, to burn superficially; also, to curve or turn round quickly or suddenly.

"I zay, meyaster, be ye gwyne to scald yer pigs, or sweal 'em?"—*i.e.*, To scald off the bristles from your pigs, or burn them off. "Hollo Jim! thee bist like a swealed cat—moore scabs than hear." "I thought I should a vared out as straaight as a line; but jest avore I got out end, that darned bwoy flung a gurt clot into hedge, and maade the wold mare sweal round; zo I ended in kind o' raainbow fashion."

SWEETWORT. The liquor of malt in brewing, before the hops are added.

SWILE. Mud or filth.

"They there pigs are up to their bellies in swile."

SWIZZLE. Small beer.

"Is that thee, Jem? I thought 'twas. Well, how dost git on wi' wold 'Billygoat'?" "Oh noohow, mayet; I shant be wi' 'en much longer, I hopes. A wants a feller to goo to plough in the aaternoon; and all we hays vor breakfast es hes wold ornery cheese, and some swizzle that's regler rot gut, as zour as vargess [verjuice]; and if a veller zays ar word, wold Billygoat 'ill putt hes boot up alongzide on 'en sharp. I sholl be middlen glad when Middlemas comes and I can get shet on't."

SWOTCHEL. To walk in a swaggering, rolling, or lazy manner.

"Wold Jack swotchels along the road as if a dedn't keer where a vell down or kept upright."

T.

Th is always pronounced *soft*, as in *thine*.

TAAIL-ON-END. Eager, hasty; to desire anything ardently, to set about anything impetuously.

"They be all taail-on-end vor't,—as ayger as a pig aater the wash bucket."

TAAILENS. Refuse corn, swept up at the tail of the "van," not saleable, and generally consumed by the farmer's household and labourers.

TAAILZORE. A disease in bullocks' tails.

TACKLE. Harness, agricultural implements; also, food or drink.

"D'ye call this treyad beer, you?" "Well, et goos vor't, mayet; but 'tes darned rum tackle to my mind."

TAFFETTY. Dainty or nice in eating; of delicate appetite.
"That maade o' mine es terbul taffetty: we can hardly git her to yet anything at all."

TAKE AATER. To be like in manner or features.
"She takes aater her mother."

TAKE VOR. To be attached to, or fond of, anyone.
"He takes vor that bwoy terribly, now hes mother's dead."

TAN. To thrash, to beat.
"I'll gee thee a pretty tannen, my lady, when I comes hooam to-night."

TANG. To make a noise with a key and a fire shovel, tea tray, or similar utensil, when bees are swarming; partly to induce them to settle—according to a popular notion, and partly to give notice to the neighbours. Also, to ring a bell; a bad taste in the mouth after something has been swallowed.
"The wold buttcher's bees be zwarmen: there's the wold dooman and the maade out in orched, maken a middlen tangen between 'em wi' the zifter and pot led, enough to frighten all the bees in the parish." "I don't like that cider, you; it leaves a terbul nasty tang in yer mouth aater ye got it down."

TAPE. A mole. (Almost obsolete.)

TARNEL. Much, great, very much.
"There's a tarnel gurt heap on't; a good deal moore than a waggon looad."

TAYKEL. A rope and pulley for lifting weights.

TEE HOLE. The hole in a bee-hive by which the bees go in and out.
"I putt my ferrets into the wheeat rick, and in vive minutes the rats zwarmed out like bees out of a tee hole."

TEENY. Small, diminutive, tiny.
"What a little teeny mite of a pig that es! Well, that es a doll pig, and noo mistake!"

TEEREN. Walking fast, in great haste.
"Hollo Bet! where bist thee teeren to?" "I be in sich a hurry, I can't stop to tell ye; there and back agen, like a man-o'-war's cruise."

TEMBER KEERT. To cart, or go with a team of horses for, timber.
"I zay, mayet, thee'st hay to be up sharp to-morrow mornen, and be off to Shawcombe vor the taykel; vor there'll be two teams on at tember keert all day to-morrow."

Tember britches. Timber breeches—a coffin.

An old man, who cousidered he suffered much from the unruly temper and tongue of his wife, in an interval of one of her upbraidings would remark: "Ah Sally, I sholl be happy one o these days, when I zees thee gwyne up over the hill in thy tember britches;"—and this unaffected ejaculation never failed to bring redoubled thunders on his devoted head.

Tend. To attend, to pretend.

"My wold dooman goos out nuss tenden now, you, and makes pretty good headway wi' et." "I never tend to plaay wi' noobody: I means what I zays."

Tender. Tinder.

"Why deary me, scores o' times avore there was any o' these lucifers about have I zet up in bed, and ben snack snacken away wi' a vlint and steel vor a quarter of an hour or moore, tryen to git a light; and then jest as I got a spark in the tender box, and putt a match too't, out 'twould goo, and I had to begin agen. 'Twas terbul tryen to anybody's temper,—specially when they happened to be in a hurry."

Terbul. Very, great, extremely; terrible. Sometimes, when special emphasis is required, pronounced "*terrábble*."

"I was terrábble bad all last week, you; I dedn't yet zixpennorth o' vittles all the time." "He's terbul fond of a bit o' minty cheese and a drop o' strong beer."

Tew. Weakly, tender, sickly.

"'That bwoy sims terbul tew vor hes age."

Thee'st. Thou hast; often used for "you have."

Then. That time.

"Git there by nine o'clock, and by then they'll be ready."

Therence. Thence, that place.

"Come out o' therence, or else I'll be aater thee."

There-right (*A.S. thœrrihte*). In that place, at once, immediately.

"Pitch in there-right."—Begin at once, in the place where you now are.

Thetch. Thatch.

Thick. Intimate, very friendly.

"They be as thick as inkle weeavers."

Thick or **Thicked' milk.** Milk thickened with flour, and boiled.

THILLER or THILL HORSE. The horse of a team which is in the shafts.

"What a beard thou hast got; thou hast got more hair on thy chin than Dobbin my thill-horse, has on his tail.
—*Merchant of Venice*, Act II. sc. 2.

THIRTOVER. Perverse, obstinate, contradictory.

"He's as thirtover as a mule; there's noo dooen nothen wi' 'en."

"Well Ben, how bist getten on, you? I hears thee'st got to git out o' that plaace o' thine, right off the reel." "That's jest about the rights on't, mayet; but 'tes darned hard lines vor a wold feller like me, what ben there zoo many years. You know you, I onny got two jackasses and a nannygoat, and the parish used to paay my rent; but zunce we had that fresh relieven officer they won't doo't noo longer, zoo I got to shift vor myself. I'd half a mind to turn rusty and stop there till they mucked me out; but then, thinks I, 'tes noo good to be thirtover about it, zo I sholl turn out."

THREADLE. To string or thread.

THUMBIT. A piece of meat eaten on a piece of bread, and so called from the thumb being placed on it.

TIDDLE. To tickle.

TIGHTISH. Pretty good, smartish, pretty well.

"He's a tightish sort o' chap to deal wi'."

TILT. The covering of a cart.

TIMERSOME. Timid, fearful.

TIME O' DAY. To "pass the time o' day," is to salute or greet a person passing by on the road.

"I can't zay I knows much about 'en, vor I onny jest passes the time o' day wi' 'en when I zees 'en."

TINES. The teeth of a harrow.

TIP OUT. To pour out anything.

"Gee us the puncheon, mayet, and let's tip out a drap o' beer."

TIPS AND CUES. Iron for the toes and heels of boots.

TISSICK. An intermittent, tickling cough.

"Strong beer cures the gout, the colic, and the tissick,
And it is for all men the very best of physic."
—*Old Song*.

Titch. To touch.
"Now then, thee buttervingered wold fool, why doesn't claa hold be et?" "Thees't better doo't thyself; I beant gwyne to titch it, I don't like the looks on't."

Titchy. Irritable, soon offended, testy.
"The wold dooman sims mortal titchy to-day."

Titty. Small, little.
"I zay, there's a little titty cat."

To-do. An upshot, an affair, a disturbance.
"Here's a pretty to-do about nothen."

To-rights. Completely, perfectly, thoroughly.
"Taailor Smith maade me a new pair o' trousers last week, and they fits to-rights, and no mistake about it." "Wold Joe Cooke was in the Barleymow, you, Zadderday night, and stripped off to fight a gipsy feller there; but the gipsy tackled 'en to-rights, and gid 'en sich a hammeren as a never had avore in his life."

Todpool. A tadpole.
"The hoss pond's vull o' tooad's spawn and todpools."

Tole. To beguile, to entice, or allure; sometimes, a relish.
"Let's git a booan, and tole the dog indoors, you."—Let us get a bone, and entice the dog indoors." "I wants a inyun or zummet, to tole down this bren cheese."—I want an onion or something, to relish this bread and cheese.

Toll-loll. Tolerably, or pretty well.

Tooad. A toad.
"'Cause I wouldn't let her run outdoors and in, and make a stabble, that maade zets there pouten and zwellen like a gurt gearden tooad; I han't got patience wi' her, I sholl let into her predney."—Because I wouldn't let her run out of doors and in, and soil the floor with her wet boots, that maid sits there pouting and swelling like a great garden toad; I haven't patience with her, and shall beat her presently.

Tooad's meat. The fungus toad's stool.

Took to. To be stopped, or taken aback; to meet with a superior.
"I thought he'd be took to zomewhen or nother."

Toppen. State, or condition of health.
"Well George, how dost sim to beat up?" "Oh, toll-loll you; how bist thee?" "Well, I han't ben over toppen vor a week or two, but there edden't much the matter it [yet]."

TOP UP. To finish a rick; to put the finishing stroke to anything.

"If we plaays in mayet, we sholl top up the rick to-night.'
"Wull ye hay any more, you?" "Oi, I'll hay a little bit o' apple pudden, jest to top up wi'."

TORE. Torn.

"There, zee what a gurt slit thee'st tore in thy smock frock."

TOSSEL. A tassel.

TOWNSER. A contemptuous name applied to an inhabitant of a town.

TOWSE. A slight blow.

"A was pretty mouthey, zo I jest gid 'en a towse in the head, and a hiked off sharp."

TRENCHER. A wooden platter.

"He's a good trencherman."—He's a hearty eater."

"He's a very valiant trencherman, he hath an excellent stomach."—*Much Ado about Nothing*, Act I., s. 1.

"Mornen, sir. I got a little bit of a passel here vor ye ; a newspaper or zummet, I louz 'tes ; but I dunno where 'tes the right one." "Thank you. Go in and tell missus to give you some bread and cheese and beer, and I'll look at the parcel while you are having it." "Thankee sir. I'll hay the beer, but I don't keer vor noo bren cheese ; I beant much of a trencherman this mornen, vor I had a good thumbit avore I started." "But this paper is not for me ; can't you read?" "Rade, sir ! I onny wish I could; I never had noo schoolen; I can't tell a gurt A vrom a bull's voot ; zometimes I takes up a paaper vor a minute or two, but I can't tell where I got'n upsidown or no, 'cepten there's a hoss in 'en, and then if the hoss's ligs be uppards I thinks he ben an rolled over ; but if I zees a house there wi' the chimley downards, then I knows I be holden the paaper upsidown."

TRENDLE (*A.S. trendel*, circle or round body). A round shallow tub, used for cooling beer.

"Cyrcle beynge rounde lyke a trendle, after the sorte as an adder lyeth."—*Hulvet*.

TREVET. An iron stand with three feet, for a pot or kettle.

TREYAD. Anything worthless or useless—trash, weeds.

"That 'ere ground is vull o' treyad." "Thee'st make theeself bad, yetten sich a lot o' wold treyad."—You will make yourself ill, eating such a lot of trash.

TREYAPSEN. To walk in a slouching or slovenly manner; to walk about to no purpose.

"My heifers be got out o' the meead, and I ben treyapsen all round the roads vor miles, but I can't zee nothen on 'em."

TRIG UP. To prop, or support; to put a stone behind the wheel of a cart to prevent its slipping back.

"Iss, I *was* bred and bornd here, and was never out o' the Island in my life it, and don't think I sholl be now. When I was young, I knowed a lot o' vokes round here that had never ben zo vur as Nippert in their lifetime, nor wouldn't goo zo vur if you'd gee 'em anything. But there, they be all dead, and things be 'tirely different now vrom what they used to be. Why, I can mind the time we onny used to goo to Nippert twice or dree times in the year, wi' a carriage o' corn; and it used to take us all day to git there and back, though we used to start at daylight. We had two teams, and always putt the bells on sich times as that. We had to trig up a time or two gwine up all the shoots; and we'd make a longish stop zometimes, if ar publichouse was handy. There,—we used to think ver' near zo much on't as people do now to goo to 'Merriky."

TROLL. To bowl a ball or a hoop; to wheel a barrow.

"Troll the wheelbarrow down into gearden."

TROLLOP. A low, dirty woman.

"I should like to zee my Joe runnen about wi' sich a trollop as she es!"

TROUNCE. To punish anyone by legal process; also, to beat.

TROW. A trough.

"Thee bist a pretty traveller! Why, thee'st never ben a mile away vrom a pig's trow in thy life."

TRUCK. Business, dealing.

"He's that sort o' a feller, that I don't want to hay noo truck wi' 'en."

TRUCKLE. To trundle, to bowl.

TUCK. To tuck a rick, is to make the sides and ends smooth, by pulling out all protruding portions.

TUCK IN. To eat; also to fit the clothes round anyone in bed.

TUCKS. Tusks of a boar.

TUNNEL. A funnel for pouring fluids into a jar or cask.

TURMETS. Turnips. The following original notice was painted on a board, and fixed in a field of turnips, by an eccentric farmer in the West of the Island, about forty years ago. A footpath ran through the field.

"Take notice.
All you people that passes by,
Take a turmet if you be dry,
And if one won't do
You may take two;
But if you takes three,
I'll take thee,
And into prison thee shalt be."

TURN. A doublo of anything, as a turn of water, two buckets full; a turn at plough, a furrow from one end of the field to the other, and back again; also, a fright or scare.

"As I was gwyne down dark layen last night, you, I zid zummet black up agen the geät pooast, and it gid me sich a turn vor a minute."

TURNEN STICKS. Long curved sticks for turning swaths of hay or corn.

TUSSLE. A contest or struggle.

TUT WORK. Work executed and paid for by the piece or lump, not by the day.

TUTTY. A nosegay, a bunch of flowers.

"And Primula, she takes the tutty there."—*Caltha Poetarum*, 1559.

TWANK. To beat or thrash. " Twanken."—A beating.

TWICKERED OUT. Tired out, very weary, done up.

"My wold dooman's ben and walked to Nippert you, and brought a tidy nitch hooam wi' her; and now aater she's ben batteren about wi' the young ones vor an hour or two, darned if she don't sim prid near twickered out." "Oi, you, noo doubt about that, but mine's a danged sight wuss; she ben to Nippert too, and rid back in Chiverton's van, but she happened to car a wold umbereller wi' her, all patched up, and wuth about drippence, what belonged to her mother, and she's come away and left 'en in zome shop or nother, and now she's got hooam she keeps on harpen about the wold thing, there's noo biden in doors long wi' her; she's wuss than a cat what's lost her kittens. She wouldn't hay noo tay, and all I can git out on her es: ' Oh dear, dear, onny to think I should a lost my poor dear wold mother's umbereller, what she had for over thirty year, I wouldn't a lost 'en vor fifty poun, noobody knows the vally I putt upon 'en but myself'; and I'll be bound I shan't hear the last on't for the next zix weeks."

TWIDDLE. To whistle; also, to trifle, to be busy about nothing.

"I heerd the robins twiddlen in copse, and that's a sign o' ranin." "The wold dooman zets in the corner o' the winder, twiddlen about wi' her knitten all day long."

TWITTER. To tremble, to be agitated.

"It upset me zoo, I be all of a twitter."

U.

UNBELIEVUN. Careless, heedless.

"That bwoy es as unbelievun as can be, 'tes noo use to zay nothen too'n."

UNBEKNOWN. Unknown.

"If a ded do anything, 'twas unbeknown to me."

UNDERGROUND. Short, thickset, undergrown.

"He's a miserable little underground sort o' feller."

UPALONG. Forwards, to go to a place.

"Well, I louz I sholl zee about gwyne upalong, you."

UP ON END. Perpendicular, upright.

"Rare the ladder up on end you, wull'ee."

UPPEN-STOCK. A horse block, a block fixed in the ground with steps for mounting a horse.

UPTIP. To overset.

"Hollo you! whoever would a thought o' zeein' thee here. How dost sim to snive?" "Oh noohow; I got the roomatics mortal bad. I got uptipped last week—keert and all—into deetch; and I had to bide there in the swile biggest part of a nower, till wold Badger come along and hauled me out on't. I'd *had* a drap, I'll own, but not enough to keep the roomatics out o' my ligs."

UPZIDES WI'. Even with, a match for, tit for tat.

"I can't be upzides wi' 'en noohow." "I'll be upzides wi' ye, bimeby, my nabs."

V.

In pronounciation, *V* is often substituted for *F*, especially in words beginning with the latter letter.

VAAIL. Progress, dispatch.
"You don't sim to make much vaail wi' your job, Tom."

VAAY. To work well, to succeed, to go smoothly.
"Things dont sim to vaay noohow to-day, to my mind."

VAIRN. Fern.

VAEG. A furious passion, a paroxysm of anger.
"He got into sich a vaeg about it."

VALL IN WI'. To coincide, to agree with; also, to meet with.
"I sholl vall in wi' et zometime or nother."—I shall meet with it sometime or other.

VALL OUT. To quarrel.

VAN. A machine for winnowing corn; also, to shake or agitate anything, so as to cause a current of air.
"Dont'ee keep on vannen the clothes zoo."

VARE OUT. To plough the first furrows of the different "lands" or "ridges" of a field.

VARM, or VARM OUT. To clean, or clean out.
"Get the dung prong, mayet, and let's varm out the steyabul.'

VANNER HAWK. The kestrel.

VENOM. Spite, ill temper.
"He spit hes venom at me."—He vented his ill-temper on me.

VETCH. To fetch.

VETTERLOCK. The fetlock.

VINNID *(A.S. fynig)*. Mouldy.
"I be terbul fond o' a bit o' blue vinnid cheese."

VIRE PAN. A fire shovel.
"I had a ham rasher in a plaet on the fender in front o' the vire, and I jest turned round to take zummet out o' cupboard, when in slips varmer Chipp's wold sheep dog and fixes my

rasher. I claaed up the vire pan and let drave at 'en, and jest kitched 'en a wipe in the ribs; but 'twas noo use, the rasher was down the keekhorn on 'en ver' near avore I looked round."

VIRE SPANNEL. A dog given to lying before the fire.

VITTEN. Proper, fitting.

VLEE. A flea, or a fly.

VLESH VLEE. The blow fly *(musca vomitoria)*.

VLITTERS. Small pancakes, fritters; also, tatters or rags.
"My smock frock is tore all in vlitters."

VLUCKER. To flutter, to fly about.

VLUX. To fly at and strike with the wings; as a hen with chickens, or sitting, will fly at an intruder.
"Don't goo in there; the wold hin's zetten, and she'll vlux ye if ye don't look out."

VOKES. Folks, people.

VOLLEY. To follow.
"What a gurt zote thing thee bist; what's keep on volleyen that maade about vor, grinnen like a dog at a rid hot coulter?"

VOOLD. An enclosure in a field for sheep, a fold; also, a foal.

VORE HOSS. The first or leading horse of a team.
"He's got the vore hoss by the head all right, I louz."—He is master of the situation—knows what he is about—has the affair well in hand.

VORERIGHT. Blundering, headstrong, regardless of consequences.
"Aye, they *ded* use to do a lot o' smugglen about here fifty or sixty year agoo, when I was a bwoy. I've heerd my father zay, one time dree or vower on 'em, wi' tubs and bags of tay, got ver' near took to by the Custom House officers, but they managed to git off the shore and into the churchyard at Niton; but zome o' the officers had slipped round another road, and prid near penned 'em in all zides. They thought 'twas a gooser wi' 'em, but one on 'em, a terbul voreright feller, called Mussel, zays: 'Come on, mayets, I be darned if I won't be upzides wi' they fellers'; zoo they prised up the stooan on one o' they gurt high brick tombs there es there, and got inside, tubs and all, and bid quiet. Cooase the officers lost 'em, and couldn't think where the deuce they was gone to, and aater searchen about a bit they went away. Zoon aaterwards, jest as 'twas gitten daylight, my father was gwyne droo the churchyard to goo to work, when all at

once he zees the stooan top o' one o' the tombs begin to move. He stopped short, and stared wi' all the eyes he'd got, when up goos the stooan higher, and a man's faace peeps out at one corner, and zays: 'I zay, mayet, can ye tell me what time 'tes?' I've heerd father zay hes hear lifted hes hat clane off hes head; a couldn't move, but stood there staren like a stuck pig; but when Mussel axed 'en what time 'twas, he roared out, and run back prid near frightened to death. He run into the vust house a come to, and zays to the people: 'Whatever wull become on us! the dead vokes in the churchyard be gitten out o' their graaves.' He was reglar terrified, and it gid 'en sich a turn he couldn't goo to work that day. Zometime aaterwards he vound out the rights on't, and he and Mussel and t'others had many a laugh about it."

VORERUNNER. An originator or beginner, an instigator.

"They two chaps was quiet enough till wold Jack must needs goo and zet 'em on, and now they be got into a pretty hobble. He was the vorerunner on't all."

VRAIL. A flail.

"I most git a new zwingel zomewhere vor my vrail."

VRITH. Cut underwood.

"We must be off down in copse vust thing to-morrow mornen mayet, vor a looad o' vrith."

VROAR. Frozen.

VULL BUTT. At full speed; also, suddenly.

"Jest as I turned the corner, I met her vull butt."— "Just as I turned the corner, I met her suddenly face to face." "Wold varmer Barton went out one sluttish aaternoon to vetch the cows, and drove 'em hooam into the backside, but a forgot to shet the geät aater'n, and goos indoors, and zets down by the vire. The cows and heifers zoon vound the geat was open, and predney out they goos all taail-o'-end, and went blaren vull butt all down the layen agen. Hes daughter was upstairs tittivaten herself longside the winder, and zid the cows run out, zo she zings out to her mother: 'Mother, where's father? The cows be all got out o' the backside, and gone to the devil, I thinks. Sholl I goo aater 'em?' 'Noa,' zed her mother, 'thee bide quiet, and I'll tell your father to goo, he's got hes spats on.'"

VURDER. Farther.

"I most zet down and hay a bit of a spell avore I can goo any vurder."

VUZ OR VUZZEN *(A.S. fyrsas)*. Furze.

Vuz-brake. Land where furze is growing.

"Last zummer, you, I was at work in varmer Morris's vuz-brake cutten a vew faggots, when all of a sudden a adder pops up and queals round my lig. I had my liggens on, zoo I jest slips my hook down and cuts my nabs in two, and went on work. Bimeby I could hear zomethin keep on cheep, cheep, like a young bird, zoo I stops a minute and went to zee what 'twas. I'm darned if that adder I cut in two wudden't there alive, and there was two moore come to look aater'n, and 'twas they that was maken the kind o' chirpen I heerd. I thought to myself I must putt a stop to these antics, zoo I zet to work and settled the hash o' the lot."

Vuz-chipper. The whin-chat, or mountain finch.

Vuz-owl. An offensive smelling insect; a kind of bug, of the *cimicidæ* family.

W.

Wad. A double wisp of hay or straw.

Waithe. Weak, languid, exhausted.

Wag *(A.S. wegan)*. To move or stir, to walk.

"I be zoo tired I can hardly wag."

"I'll work wi' my broad axe as long as I can wag."
—*Old Song.*

Want. A mole. "Want ketcher."—A mole catcher.

Wanty. A chain or girth attached to the shafts of a cart or waggon, and passing under the horse's belly.

Warm. To beat or thrash.

"I'll gee thee a good warmen when I ketches thee."

War'nt. To warrant.

"I zay mayet, if thee keeps tunnen the beer into thee like that, thee'st be swipey avore nammet time."—"I'll war'nt it you."

"My wold granfer used to live at Gatcombe, and plaayed the clarinet, or hobwoy, or zummet like it in church; he used to plaay, and the clark and two or dree more used to zing, and that was all the music they had. Wold Dr. Wusley [Worsley] I thinks was paason then, and lived at Pidford, and Squire Campbell or zomebody or nother lived at Gatcombe gurt house. Zunday mornens the Squire used to goo to church, and the Doctor always used to waait vor'n, and never maade a start till he was in hes zetten. I've heerd the wold man tell the story many a time. One Zunday Dr. Wusley wudden't at hooam, and a fresh paason come to do duty. Of course, he wudden't up to the ins and outs on't, and when the bell stopped he pitched off direckly wi' 'When the wicked man'—but the clark jumped up and zays, 'Stop a bit zur, he edden't come in it!' It maade the paason stare a bit, I'll war'nt it."

WARNUT. A walnut.

WARP. To cast a foal.

"My mare's warped her voold."

WASHTUB. A tub to contain wash, *i.e.*, pot-liquor and kitchen refuse for pigs.

WATER-GEAL. A second or double rainbow appearing above the first.

WATSHED. Wet in the feet, wetshod.

"Be got ar bit watshed, you, gwyne athirt the brook?"

"For weet-shoed thei gone."—*Piers Plowman.*

WEATH. Flexible, pliant, supple.

WEEAZE. A wad, or wisp of hay or straw.

"There's noo moore in 'en than there es in a wet weeaze."

WI' 'EN. With him. "Wi' 'er."—With her. "Wi't."—With it. (The *i* pronounced as *ee.*)

WELT. To beat severely.

"I'll gee thee sich a welten as thee'st never had in thee life, if thee doesn't mind what I tells thee."

WEX. Wax.

"Od zooks I've lost my wex,
Whatever es become on't!
'Tes enough to make a man vex,
Here lays a leetle crumb on't."
—*Old Song.*

WEYSAN. Thin.

WHIPPENCE. A spreader, or bar, for yoking two or more horses to a plough or harrow.

WHIPSWHILE. Now and again, frequently.

"I dunno what there med be between 'em, but he's there every whipswhile."

WHISTERSNIFF. A slap, a backhanded blow.

"'The wold dooman gid me sich a whistersniff in the chops."

WHITE RICE. The white beam, *pyrus aria*.

WHITE WOOD. The lime tree.

WHOP. Weight, force; also, a heavy blow.

"'Tes miserable slippery this mornen; I hadn't got out doors half a minute, avore down I come wi' sich a whop, right on my zide, I thought I had broke my yarm."

WHUP. A word used to tell horses to stop.

"Hoot, touch up Pedlar! Knock down Captain! Joit off Drummer! Whup! whup! whup!"

Thirty years ago an old labourer when at plough used to make the field ring with the above rhythmic ejaculations, delivered in stentorian tones that could be heard at least a quarter of a mile off; and so often, that all the ploughboys in the neighbourhood had them by heart, and frequently shouted them in the hearing, and to the annoyance, of their original utterer.

WIGGLE. To twist about, to wriggle, to move continually.

WICKER. To neigh, or whinny, as a horse.

WILLEY *(A.S. wilie)*. A large basket for carrying chaff, &c.

WIM. To winnow.

WIMSHEET. A large piece of sail cloth, or a sail, used in barns; a winnowing sheet.

WINDY. Wheedling, deceitful, insinuating.

"That wold jobber wanted to git they pigs out o' me terbul bad, and wudden't he jest about windy over it; but 'twas noo good, I could zee droo it, he was too flitch by half."

WITH. A twisted wand of willow or hazel, used to bind faggots, &c.

WITHOUT. Unless, except.

"I shan't goo without he goos too."

WITHY. The willow; various species of *salix*.

WITHYBED. A plantation of withies, or ground where withies are growing.

"When I was a youngish chap I was at work in a withybed t'other zide o' Aaton out at Freshwater, rather acarly in the mornen, and I zid a wold man lerruppen along the road, and every now and ten stoppen and glaren all round as if a couldn't make out where a was got to. Predney a come up auverright me, and makes a stop, and a zays, 'Hollo mayet, what plaace do ye call this?' I thought a was about half sprung, zo I zed too'n, 'This plaace is a withybed, as ver as I knows.' 'My eyes,' zays the wold feller, 'I can't maake noo fist on't at all, that's the saame neyam as they calls it in the Isle o' Wight.' Hearen this, maade *me* open my eyes pretty wide vor a minute. 'Well, drat thee,' I zays too'n, 'Where dost think thee bist then?' 'Where I be,' a zed, 'why this es France, edden't it?' 'Why, ye zoat wold man,' I zays, 'thee bist out on't all together, this is Freshwater.' 'If this edden't the head goo of all I ever zid in my life,' zays the wold feller, 'if there edden't a plaace called the saame in the Island, and 'tes jest sich a plaace as this es.' I couldn't stand noo moore of his wold zoat foolishness, I got that mad wi'n. 'Ye muddle headed wold fool,' I zays too'n, 'thee most be drunk or craazy; and I beleeves thee knows thee way about as well as I do, vor I can tell by thee talk thee bist a Isle o' Wighter, and I've zid thee avore to day zomewhere; goo long hooam and putt thee head in a bag till thee gits sober, or else thees't zoon vind thyself in Bedlam.' 'I was never zoo putt to in my life, I can't make it out at all,' a zed, and on a went. I was talken about the wold fool a vew days aaterwards, and I heerd a was wold Manny Young, a kind o' feller that used to do anything, and led about in lotes and barns where a could, all over the Island. The night avore I zid 'en, he'd ben helpen to land zome tubs at Totland Bay, and got too much liquor into'n, and slept in a booat on the shore aater they'd clewed up, till mornen. When a turned out at daylight, zome on' em toold 'en they'd shoved off and got back agen in the night while he was asleep, and was jest now landed in France. The wold man zed he was never there avore, and he *should* like above everything now a *was* there to hay a bit of a walk round jest to zee the country. Zoo a swotcheld off on the road to Freshwater, and avore a got vur, he thought he'd zid a plaace terbul much like it zomewhere; zoo a axed everybody a met (and 'twudden't many at that time o' the mornen) where a was; but mooast on 'em onny laughed at 'en, so the vurder a went the more a got hoped up over it; but aater a left me and got on ver near to Wellow, a vound out the rights on't, and that a was in the Island aater all."

WOBBLE. To move from side to side unevenly, to shake or oscillate.

WOLD. Old. A word much used as a prefix in conversation, as the "Wold man," "Wold dooman," "Wold farmer Smith," "Wold cobbler Coombes," &c.

WOLLUP. To beat or thrash.

WOODQUEST. A wood-pigeon. (Almost obsolete.)

WOOT. Will you? "Wooten't."—Will you not?

Wopse. A wasp. "Wopses."—Wasps.
"Come on chaps, let's goo and zwarm this wopses' nest."

To *zwarm* a "wopses'" nest—*i.e.*, to burn out or destroy one—is a serious undertaking among boys; and the operation being attended with some risk and danger, those foremost in the affair are regarded as heroes by their fellows.

Wordle. The world.
"I couldn't do sich a thing vor the wordle."

Wrench. To sprain.
"I beleeve I've wrenched my lig, jumpen off the mow."

Wropped. Creased, rumpled.
"My shirt front es all wropped up like a dish clout."

Wurret. To fret, to plague, or tease.
"She wurrets herself about it terbul." "How they vlees do wurret the dog, to be sure!"

Wurt. A wart.
"What a crop of wurts thee *hast got* on thee hands Bob! Now, if you'll onny goo down to wold taailor Young, and stand 'en a pint, he'll charm 'em all away in a day or two."

Wuts. Oats. "Wut ben."—The bin in which oats are kept for the horses in a stable.
"I zay, mayet, let's hay a geeam o' mariners, there is a boord cut out on the led of the wut ben."

Wuzbird. A term of reproach, usually applied to boys only; of no definite meaning, but probably a corruption of *whore's bird*.
"Come out o' that, ye young wuzbird, or I'll git a stick and prid near cut ye in two."

Y.

Yallow-bwoys. Sovereigns, or guineas.
"Wold Dannel Keach was a regler lantern jaad wold bachelor, and I thinks he haated the very sight o' childern. He was in varmer Barton's one time hayen a pipe and a glass o' grog wi' 'em, and they had there dree or vower as fine looken bwoys growen up as you could zee in a day's march. As they was zetten by the vire, missus, woman-like, zays to Dannel,

'Shouldn't you like, Mister Keach, to hay sich a lot of bwoys as we got, zetten round your chimley at hooam?' 'Noa,' zed Dannel, 'that's jest what I *shouldn't* like; I'd zooner hay dree or vower yallow-bwoys in my pocket any time than all the lot on 'em.' Missus couldn't stand Dannel aater that."

YALLOW-CALL (sometimes YALLOW-CUP). The crow's foot, *Ranunculus arvensis*. The "Tufted crow-toe" of Milton: *Lycidas*.

YALLOW-JANDERS. The jaundice.

YAP. To yelp, or bark like a dog.

"I could hear the dog keep on yap, yappen."

YARM. The arm.

YENDER. Yonder.

"Casn't zee that tree out yender?"

YEPPERN. An apron.

" Thee gurt zote mud, thee bist onny fit to be tied to thee grammer's yeppern string."

"I zay, Jim, jest look'ee, here's a lot o' wold paainters comen along the road, wi' zome wold dooman's yepperns on."

YET. To eat; ate, or eaten.

"I han't got a mossel o' bread in house: 'twas all yet up at dinnertime."

An old labourer of the writer's acquaintance was terribly puzzled with the word *yet*. He had joined the "Bryanites," and for the first time in his life took to reading the Bible. He began of course at the beginning, and in due time arrived at Genesis, chap. xlv., and the last verse, containing the joyful exclamation of the patriarch Jacob, on his being satisfied that his long lost son Joseph was alive and well. " Joseph my son is *yet* alive, I will go and see him before I die." "Now," argued the old man, "I always ben toold, and I bleeves it, that the Bible es true. But there's a hatch zomewhere in this story, vor however could wold Jacob zee hes son Joseph if hee'd ben *yet alive?* If hee'd ben *yet* up alive, or dead, how could there be any on 'en left vor his father to zee? That's what I wants to know." It was only after some time and trouble spent in copious explanation of the totally different significations of *yet* and *eat*, that the old man pronounced himself fully satisfied; but this was the only difficult passage he met with in the whole of the Pentateuch.

YO. An ewe.

YOPPUL. Useless talk, incessant gabble.

"Dedn't the wold dooman yoppul at us!"

"It used to be a terbul out-o'-the-way plaace here by St. Cattern's, and zome rum fellers used to live here years agoo, avore I can mind, but I've heerd tell on 'em a good many times. Wold Dove (he or his brother used to keep the Star at Niton years agoo), was a miserable ignorant, voreright sort o' feller, and when a got woldish a'd zet mumchanced in the chimley corner vor half a day together; but if anybody ded git or a word or two out on 'en, 'twas zummet to the pwynt, pend upon't. He was mortal bad vor a long time, and they thought he'd zoon slip his wind; zoo they got the paason to come and zee what he could make on 'en. Zo the paason come and begun talken too'n, but the wold man zet and zed nothen for zome time. I'redney the paason axed 'en, 'Do ye know who maade ye?' Then wold Dove opened his jaas and zays, 'Noa, I dunno as I do, dost thee?' 'Iss,' zed the paason, 'I do—God Almighty; don't ye bleeve it?' 'I beant nooway sarten about it,' zays wold Dove, 'vor all I got to goo by is what I ben toold about it, and vokes always zays ye most never bleeve half o' what ye hears; zoo shet up and don't let me hay noo moore o' yer yoppul.' 'Come here Jin,' a zung out to hes wife, 'I be got as hungerd as a hoss; cut us off a bit o' that choppekin ye bwiled yesterday, wull'ee.'"

YOU. A word much used in familiar talk, as "I zay, you, I lowz 'twull raain avore long." "Oi, you, zoo do I." "What time is it, you?" "What's think o' that you?" &c.

YOURN. Yours.

"If that rake edden't yourn, it most be ourn."

YOWL. To yelp, or howl like a dog.

Z.

In the pronunciation of many words beginning with S and Z the initial letters are often interchanged, as *zence* for *sence*; *sim* or *zim*, for *seem*; *sich* or *zich*, for *such*; *zay* or *say*, for *sea*; *sweal* or *zweal*, to *scorch*; &c.

ZAAMER. To loiter, to saunter, to walk in a lazy manner.

"I expected 'en here jest aater dinner, but a dedn't come; but a zaamered downalong about dree o'clock."

ZAW. A saw; or to saw.

ZEED-LIP. A box to contain corn for sowing, suspended by a strap from the sower's shoulder.

ZEE'N. See him. ZEE'T. See it.
"Casn't zee't, you?" "Noa, I can't zee ar one here."

ZET AT. To abuse, to scold, or rate soundly.

ZET OFF. To start, to go; also, to explode gunpowder.

ZET OUT. An upshot, a disturbance; also, a feast or merry-making.
"Here's a pretty zet out! The pump's all vroze up, and I can't get a drap o' water." "I zay you, wold Bob Cook's maade es run away long wi' a sojer, and there's the deuce of a zet out about it." "We be gwyne to hay a anniversary at our chapel, Whitmonday. There'll be plenty of tay and cake about, and a fine zet out I louz."

ZET UP. To be insubordinate or refractory; also, to stand the pins up at the game of "Four corners," or skittles.
The following original epistle, which exemplifies the use of "Zet up," was sent by an Island churchwarden, who was also a brewer or publican, to his parish overseer in 1792:—
"To Mister ——
"As I be suppaned to goo to Lunnon as a witnes in the King's name, I desier you not to releave no parpers with the parrish munny without thare passes, and if they zets up about it, call in the cunstable direckly. But if anny of our own poor applies to you, tell em if they drinks no tay, and keeps no doggs for poachen, I wont forgit em next Crismas.—Yours &c., ——."

ZETTEN DOWN. To give anyone a good "zetten down," is to rebuke them very sharply, or to teach them their place.

ZIDELEN. Sloping, slanting, the sloping side of a hill.

ZIDLE. To edge, to squeeze, or sneak in.
"He zidled in jest now, and zet hisself down in the corner, looken rather queer."

ZIFTER PAN. A fire shovel.

ZINDERS. Cinders.

ZIPPET (sometimes SIPPET). A small sop or toast.

ZIVE *(A.S. sithe)*. A scythe.

ZIVE-SNEAD. The pole or handle of a scythe.
"I went to Whittle t'other night you, to the blacksmith's,

to git the ring fitted to my zive-snead, and while the job was dooen I went across the road vor a bit, and heerd the paason gee a lecter 'bout moral improvement." "Well, what ded'st think on't?" "Oh, 'twas all very well as vur as I knows." "Oi you, we all knows that *marl do* improve the ground wonderful."

ZOMEWHEN. Some time, any time.

ZOOL. A stake or shore, driven into the ground, to which the hurdles in a sheepfold are fastened.

ZOOZAY. For the occasion, for the sake of talking.

"I don't take the least notice of what that wold dooman talks about, she only doos it vor a zoozay. There's no bottom in her."

ZOTE or ZOAT. Silly, soft, foolish. (*Spanish—zote*) an ignorant or lazy person.

"What a gurt zote thing thee bist."

ZOTEY. An idiot, a fool.

ZULL *(A.S. syl).* A plough.

"Come on zotey, and take hold o' the zull, while I takes up a hole or two."

ZUMMER FRECKLED. Spots on the face caused by the heat of the sun.

ZUNCE. Since.

"I han't a zid nothen on 'en zunce dinnertime."

ZWALLEY. To swallow; also, to believe, or give credit to.

"I zay varmer, d'ye think we be gwyne to hay another 'lection avore the year's out?" "I'm sure I can't zay; I hears a tarnel deal o' talk about politics and 'lections, but I don't zwalley it all, and 'twull make very little difference to any on us here, let it be how 'twull." "Well I don't zee why we should trouble ourselves over it; one time we *ded* use to git a dinner, and plenty o' grog aaterwards, but there edden't a mote nor drap o' nothen to be got now, and I nooways zees the fun o' gwyne two or dree mile to vote on a leer stummick." "Oi you, they be all vor their own ends, and to my mind 'tes zummet anewse like this wi' the Liberals and Tories, booath on 'em. My wold zow got a straain o' ten pigs, and they can't all zuck at once, vor one thing she han't got toats enough, and bezides there edden't room vor 'em all together, zoo I shets vour or vive on 'em out o' the sty while t'others be zucken, and they that be shet out keeps on runnen round and squeeken, and kicks up a mortal to do till they be let in agen, and then they be quiet enough, I warn't it." "Haw,

haw, that's jest about the rights on't, and how they *do* goo on; I can't rade in noo sense myzelf, but missus rades the paaper to me in evenens, and vrom what I can make on't, these Conservatives sims to be about the best on 'em, zoo I sholl gee 'em a vote next time, but I always *have* voted vor the Tories up to now."

ZWARM. To swarm, as bees; also, to beat or thrash.

"Wold Joe rined off, and zwarmed into'n like one o'clock."

"If thee dosn't shet up thy mouth, I'll zwarm into thee in a minute or two."

ZWAUTH *(A.S. swœthe)*. A layer or row of grass or corn, after being cut down by a scythe.

ZWIFTER. Part of the tackling that fastens a load of timber to the waggon.

ZWIMMER. A thin, circular pudding, made of flour and water, put into the pot while the other contents are cooking, and being soon ready, is taken out, cut open, buttered, and eaten for lunch.

"'Twun't be dinnertime avore one o'clock, and I sims terbul leer; zo let's hay a zwimmer, missus."

ZWINGEL. The part of the flail which falls upon the corn in threshing, fastened to the "handstaff" by a wooden swivel and strips of raw hide.

ZWIVETTY. Giddy; feeling of vertigo, or swimming in the head.

The PLAY acted by the "CHRISTMAS BOYS," in the Isle of Wight.

In many parts of England and Wales, a rude kind of drama used to be performed at Christmas, chiefly in the rural districts, by mummers in various characters and disguises; but during the last forty or fifty years the custom has gradually been falling into desuetude, and at present is seen but very rarely. The characters vary in different localities, but a large portion of the text of the play is everywhere substantially the same; and as a whole bears much more resemblance to the mysteries or moralities of the Middle Ages (from which it is probably derived), than to a modern drama.

Without claiming for the play an origin as ancient as the time of the Crusades, "mumming" at Christmas was popular in England in the fourteenth century, and persons of rank often took part in the performance. Some of the characters as now represented are of considerable antiquity, being probably more or less derived from Richard Johnson's "*Famous History of the Seven Champions of Christendom*"; published in the latter part of the reign of Queen Elizabeth.

The performers sometimes introduced allusions to contemporary events, and personations of the popular hero, or notability of the day, which caused curious anachronisms. Alexander the Great, Bonaparte, Lord Nelson, Hector, and the King of Egypt jostled each other on the stage, and were mixed together in the representation. Lord Nelson and Bonaparte were sometimes introduced as characters in the play as performed in the Island early in the present century, but Hector and Alexander were never seen there, being generally found only in versions of the drama as given in the midland and northern counties of England. The following version of the play as represented in the Island forty or fifty years ago, is derived from two copies in MS. (one of older date than the other), verbal relations, and the writer's own recollections. It is evident that by "King" George, *Saint* George is meant; *King* probably taking the place of *Saint*, some time after the accession of the House of Hanover to the English throne; and in all likelihood the original title or name of the production was—" The Christmas Play, or Pageant of St. George." The performers were generally young men of the neighbourhood, who, during the Christmas holidays, perambulated their own and adjoining parishes, exhibiting in the houses of the gentry and principal persons; and a performance open to all comers, at the Village Inn, generally finished each evening. A collection was made at the conclusion, and the proceeds divided among the players, who often liquidated the greater part of their gains before they separated.

DRAMATIS PERSONÆ.

GREAT HEAD AND BLUNDER; this part often taken by
    POOR AND MEAN.
KING GEORGE.
THE NOBLE CAPTAIN.
THE TURKISH KNIGHT.
THE VALIANT SOLDIER.
THE DOCTOR.
FATHER CHRISTMAS. JOHN BULL, generally the same.
MOTHER CHRISTMAS.
FATHER OF TURKISH KNIGHT; sometimes played by
    FATHER CHRISTMAS.
POOR AND MEAN.

Father and Mother Christmas appear in old great coats, the latter wearing an old bonnet and skirt. They walk in bending, and as if decrepid through age, with the backs of their coats well stuffed with straw. This is necessary, as during the performance they furiously belabour each other, Father Christmas wielding a cudgel, and Mother Christmas a formidable broom. " Poor and Mean" appears in tattered habiliments; " The Doctor " in a rusty black coat and wig; the " Valiant Soldier " in an old red uniform coat; the " Turkish Knight " wears a turban, and has generally a good deal of green in his attire; "King George" is resplendent in a shining helmet and a coat covered with gold spangles; the "Noble Captain" often sports a cocked hat and a blue coat; and the dresses of most of the players are profusely bedecked with tinsel and ribbons of different colours according to their fancy.

Enter GREAT HEAD AND BLUNDER.
Here comes I—Gurt Head and Blunder,
If I bean't a fool edden't that a wonder,
Move all your chairs and taables and jint stools,
Vor behind me there comes a pack o' fools;
But if you don't like to hear what I've got to zay,
Step in my braave King George, and clear the way.
Exit, enter KING GEORGE.
Room, room, ye gallyants, room,
And gimme room to rhyme;
I be come to show you my activity
All on this Crismus time.
I've acted youth, I've acted age,
The like was never zid avore, or acted on this stage;
But if you won't listen to what I've got to zay,
Step in wold Father Crismus, and clear the way.
Exit, and enter old FATHER CHRISTMAS.
Here comes I—wold Father Crismus,
Welcome, or welcome not,
And I hopes wold Father Crismus
Wull never be forgot.
As I don't come onny once a year,
We should all like to taaste your wold strong beer;
And now I'm come I han't got long to stay,
But my sons and I wull make a little spoort
Avore we goos away.
Zo ladies and gentlemen gimme room,
Vor room o' you I praay,
And I'll call in the Noble Captain to clear the way.
Exit, enter the NOBLE CAPTAIN.
Here be I—the Noble Captain,
Jest returned across the say:
My naame it es the Noble Captain,
You med a heerd zome talk o' me.
Vust—I fout in France,
Second—I fout in Spain,
And now I be come to England
To fight King George again,
Or any of his men; I, and one moore,
Fout and beät twenty score;
Twenty score, all mighty men,
And now I'm here to beät as many moore.
Enter VALIANT SOLDIER.
Here comes I—the Valiant Sojer,
And Bold Slasher es my naame.
I'm jest returned vrom Denmark,
For 'twas there I gaained my fame;
And wi' my soord and trusty spear
I hopes to win the geame.
Many's a battle have I ben in

    To sarve King George, our noble king.
    I've fout by say, I've fout by land,
    Until I could no longer stand.
NOBLE CAPTAIN.
    What little prattlen tongue es this I hears?
VALIANT SOLDIER.
    Not sich a prattlen tongue as you med think, mounseer.
NOBLE CAPTAIN.
    I'll fight thee like a lion, or an oak.
VALIANT SOLDIER.
    A man of British heart thou dost provoke.
                        They cross swords and fight.
NOBLE CAPTAIN.
    Provoke! I zay I despise the heart o' thee.
Enter JOHN BULL *with a club, he strikes down their swords.*   *Exeunt*
        NOBLE CAPTAIN *and* VALIANT SOLDIER.
JOHN BULL.
    Here be I—wold John Bull,
    If they hadn't zoon ben gone
    I'd gid 'em boath a bellyvull.
    And if you won't listen to what I've got to zay,
    Step in the Turkish Knight, and clear the way.
        Exit JOHN BULL, *and enter* TURKISH KNIGHT.
    Here comes I the Turkish Knight,
    In the Turkish land I've learned to fight;
    I'll fight King George and all his min,
    And taame their courage bold;
    And if his blood be ever zo hot
    I'll quickly make it coold.
    Oh! if I had him here,
    What works there would appear;
    I'd hag him, I'd jag him,
    I'd cut him as small as a fly,
    I zend him to zome far land
    To make a Crismus pie.
            Enter KING GEORGE.
    Here comes I—King George,
    That man of courage bold,
    And with my soord and spear
    I've won ten crowns o' gold.
    I fout the viery dragon
    And brought him to gurt slaughter,
    And by the meeans o' that I won
    The King of Egypt's daughter.
            Crosses swords with TURKISH KNIGHT.
    Neither unto thee am I bound to bend,
    Vor I never took thee to be my friend.
TURKISH KNIGHT.
    Why sir—did I ever do you any harm?

KING GEORGE.
You did, you saucy cock, so begone.
TURKISH KNIGHT.
A saucy cock!—call me that naame agen,
I'll stab thy heart, or any o' thy men. *Lunges.*
KING GEORGE.
A stab, sir, not the least I fear,
Jest naame the plaace, I'll meet thee there.
TURKISH KNIGHT.
Across the water—the hour o' vive.
KING GEORGE.
I'll meet thee there, if I be alive.
TURKISH KNIGHT.
Across the water—the hour o' ten,
I'll meet thee there wi' vour score men.
KING GEORGE.
With all my heart it sholl be done,
A loven couple do agree
To fight the battle manfully. *They fight.*
TURKISH KNIGHT.
I'll hag thee, I'll jag thee,
I'll cut thee as small as a fly,
I'll zend thee to zome far land
To make a Crismus pie.
KING GEORGE.
Mince pies hot, and mince pies coold,
I'll zend thee to the devil avore thee bist dree days wold.
The drums do beät, the trumpets sound,
At the word o' command, the battle's begun ;
The battle fout in this castle is won.
Thrusts the TURKISH KNIGHT *through, who falls.*
Oh zee, oh zee what I have done,
I've cut him down like the evenen zun ;
And now I've slain this Turkish Knight,
Ten thousand moore sich men I'd fight,
All to maintain wold England's right.
Enter OLD MAN.
Oh thou cursed and cruel Christian,
Jest zee what thou hast done,
Thou hast ruined me by killen o' my son.
KING GEORGE.
Wold Age, Wold Age, I did him kill
My honour to maintain,
Vor if I hadn't sarr'd him zo
He would a sarr'd me the saame.
He vust gid me the challenge
And how could I deny,
I cut the buttons off his cooat
And zee there low he lies.
Exit KING GEORGE.

OLD MAN.
   Es there ar skilful doctor to be vound
   To cure my son's most deadly wound?
                  Enter DOCTOR.
   Oh iss—there es a very skilful Doctor to be vound
   To cure the sick and make 'em sound,
   And raise the dead up off the ground.
OLD MAN.
   What canst thee cure, Doctor?
DOCTOR.
   The itch, the stitch, the palsy, and the gout;
   Pains within, and pains without;
   And if there was nineteen devils in this man
   I'd zoon vetch twenty out.
OLD MAN.
   Well then, cure my belovèd son
   That on the ground do lay,
   And let thy charge be what it wull
   The sum to thee I'll paay.
                  Exit OLD MAN.
DOCTOR.
   Here be I—little Doctor Good,
   And in my hands lays that man's blood.
   If he'd ben dead zix weeks or moore,
   To him his life I could restore.
   I've got a little bottle in my waistcoat pocket
   Called Hokum, Smokum, Alecumpane;
   If I jest putts a little drop on this man's cheek,
   He'll rise and boldly fight agen.
Drops some fluid on the TURKISH KNIGHT'S *face, who opens his eyes,
              and rises.*
                  Enter OLD MAN.
   Oh thou skilful Doctor, what is thy fee?
DOCTOR.
   Ten pound is usually my fee,
   But twenty I demand of thee.
                  Exeunt OLD MAN *and* DOCTOR.
TURKISH KNIGHT.
   How long have I laid bleeden in this bloody gore?
   I've ben cut and slashed vrom sore to sore,
   I thought I'd fout enough avore,
   But now I be rose agen—I'll fight as many more.
                  Enter VALIANT SOLDIER.
   What little prattlen tongue is this I hears?
TURKISH KNIGHT.
   Not sich a prattlen tongue as you med think, mounseer.
VALIANT SOLDIER.
   If you don't hold your little prattlen tongue
   I'll sar thee wuss than any avore have done.

TURKISH KNIGHT.
> With all my heart it sholl be done,
> A loven couple do agree
> To fight the battle manfully.

They fight, and the VALIANT SOLDIER *strikes the* TURKISH KNIGHT *to his knees.*

Enter KING GEORGE. *The* TURKISH KNIGHT *on his knees offers him his sword.*

TURKISH KNIGHT.
> King George, King George, one thing of thee I crave,
> Grant me my life, I'll be thy faithful slave.

KING GEORGE.
> Arise, arise, you Turkish dog,
> To Turkey go agen,
> And tell them what brave champions
> Wold England do maintain.

Exeunt VALIANT SOLDIER *and* TURKISH KNIGHT.

> And now I've ended what I had to zay,
> Step in my Noble Captain, and clear the way.

Enter the NOBLE CAPTAIN.

> Here comes I, the Noble Captain,
> Jest returned vrom over the say;
> I be called the Noble Captain,
> Ye most have heerd o' me.
> Vust I fout in France,
> Then I fout in Spain,
> I've fout the Valiant Sojer,
> And now I be come to do't agen.
> I'll fight King George, or any of his men,
> I never fight one man, but always ten.
> I'll fight ye all, boath big and small,
> And putt your King to flight;
> Vor I be come a purpose vor to fight.
> My head is maade o' iron,
> My body is maade o' steel,
> My ligs be maade o' paven stooans,
> No soord can make me veel.

Enter KING GEORGE.

> Come forth thou foreign dog—to thee I say,
> Pull out thy soord and fight,
> Pull out thy puss and pay,
> Vor satisfaction I wull have
> Avore I goos away.

NOBLE CAPTAIN.
> No puss wull I pull out,
> No money wull I pay,
> But satisfaction I'll have o' thee
> Avore I goos away.

KING GEORGE.
> With all my heart it sholl be done,

A loven couple do agree
To fight the battle manfully.
They fight, and KING GEORGE *runs the* NOBLE CAPTAIN *through, who falls on his face.*
O Doctor, Doctor, come in haste,
The Noble Captain lies bleeding on his face.
Enter DOCTOR, *who after repeating the same words, and a similar performance with the* NOBLE CAPTAIN *as before with the* TURKISH KNIGHT, *the* NOBLE CAPTAIN *rises and goes out.*

DOCTOR.
And now I've ended what I had to zay,
Come in wold Mother Crismus, and clear the way.
Enter MOTHER CRISMUS *with an old broom.*

MOTHER CHRISTMAS.
Here comes I that han't ben it,
Wi' my gurt head and little wit;
My head is big and my body small,
But I'll do my best to plaise you all.
Begins to sweep.
Sweep, sweep, all I vinds I sholl keep.
Enter FATHER CHRISTMAS.
How dare thee to sweep in my house?

MOTHER CHRISTMAS.
How comes it to be thy house?

FATHER CHRISTMAS.
My sons and I fout vor'n.

MOTHER CHRISTMAS.
Where ded ye fight vor'n?

FATHER CHRISTMAS.
In England, Ireland, France, and Spain,
And now I be come back I'll fight wold smut agen.
They fight with cudgel and broom, till KING GEORGE *enters and turns them out.*

KING GEORGE.
And now we've nearly ended our fine play
I'll call in Poor and Mean to clear the way.
Enter POOR AND MEAN.
Here comes I—wold Poor and Mean,
And hardly worthy to be seen,
Roast beef, plum pudden and Crismus pie,
Who likes that better than my sons and I!
A jug o' your good Crismus ale
Wull make us dance and zing,
And money in our pockets is a very fine thing;
Now all o' you ladies and gennelmen that have
Heerd my sons' voices ring,
Jest drap a vew hapence in my wold hat,
And you shall hear us zing,
God save the Queen.
(Songs generally follow ad lib.)

NOTES.

In the oldest MS. copy of the play collated for the foregoing version, the following lines occur in the first speech of the " Valiant Soldier."

> " We surrounded Copenhagen—
> Our Admiral by sea, and our General on land,
> We drove them from the city, and they could no longer stand,
> Our sailors have beaten them again and again,
> And our soldiers as before will behave like men."

These lines must have been introduced early in the present century, and evidently refer, not to the Battle of Copenhagen fought by Nelson in 1801, but to the bombardment of that city in 1807 by Lords Gambier and Cathcart.

Sometimes at the discretion of the players, but not very often, instead of " John Bull " entering and striking down the swords of the " Valiant Soldier " and the " Noble Captain " when fighting, a character was substituted called " Old Bendozer," who enters with a club and delivers himself as follows:

> " Here comes I—wold Bendozer,
> If they hadn't slipped off when they ded
> I'd gid 'em boath a closer."

This is a curious example of the introduction of a contemporary celebrity, as " Bendozer " is a palpable corruption of the name Mendoza, borne by a noted Jew pugilist, at the end of the last, and beginning of the present, century.

In the older MS. of the play, before quoted, instead of " King George" fighting the " Noble Captain," he encounters " Bonaparte."

> *Enter* BONAPARTE.
> " Here am I—great Bonaparte,
> The Emperor of the French,
> In many a battle I have been
> And never fled an inch;

> I was in Trafalgar Bay, and the battle of Waterloo,
> And now I'm come to England to show you what I can do.
> I am valiant and of great might,
> And come here on purpose for to fight,
> I'll fight you all both great and small
> And put your King to flight," &c., &c.

proceeding in similar words to those used by the "Noble Captain."

> *Enter* KING GEORGE.
> "Thou French dog,
> Pull out thy sword and fight," &c., as before.
> *They fight, and* KING GEORGE *runs* BONAPARTE *through.*

The Doctor appears and revives Bonaparte, who gets on his legs and says:

> "And now I'm rose, I'll just go on my way."
> *The* DOCTOR *collars him.*
> "No, no, you dog, you don't, before you pay.
> I never was served such a dirty trick before,
> And after all my pains,—get out, outside the door."
> *Kicks* BONAPARTE *out.*

A character sometimes represented or omitted, at the pleasure of the performers, is "Beelzebub," whose part generally consists but of four lines:

> "Here comes I—old Bellzebub,
> And on my shoulder I carries my club,
> And in my hand a dripping pan,
> Now don't you think me a jolly old man?"

Another character, but very seldom introduced, is "Little Johnny Jack."

> "Here comes I—little Johnny Jack,
> With my wife and family at my back;
> Although I looks so young and small,
> I'm the biggest rogue among them all."

AN ISLAND "HOOAM HARVEST."

"HOOAM HARVEST," or Harvest Home, as formerly celebrated, is now become a thing of the past, and lives only in the memory of a generation also fast passing away. Forty or fifty years ago it was kept in much the same style as from time immemorial, or as far back as the recollections of the "oldest inhabitant" reached; but then principally by the smaller farmers cultivating from 100 to 200 acres, who kept most of their men "in house," and supplied their "hands" with meat and drink during the "harvest month," following the customs of their fathers. The festivity of Harvest Home, and providing a supper for the farm labourers and servants of the farmer's household at the end of harvest, dates from the remotest antiquity, and was established in England for many generations before it was noted by Hentzner, who in the narrative of his journey into England in the year 1598, says: "As we were returning to our inn, we happened to meet some country people celebrating their Harvest Home. Their last load of corn they crown with flowers." Often, during the harvest month, on the conclusion of wheat or barley cart, the evening was ended after supper with songs, and an extra pint or two of strong beer was served all round to the labourers; the whole proceeding being a kind of rehearsal or foretaste of the real "Hooam Harvest," which crowned and concluded the labours of the month. All the labourers and extra men were engaged at so much for the "harvest month," and were provided with meat and drink during that time by the farmer, faring the same as his yearly servants engaged from Michaelmas to Michaelmas. On very busy days during harvest, if a field wanted clearing, or a rick to be finished in a given time, the carpenter and blacksmith who did the farm work came willingly with their apprentices and lent a hand, and were always invited to the Home Harvest supper as an acknowledgment.

The last load of the harvest being on the waggon, a "puncheon" of "nammet beer" was generally drunk round it in the field, and with green boughs stuck on the top, it proceeded, generally accompanied with cheering, to the "rickess." In the meantime the farmer's wife, with her maids, and help extraordinary from a neighbour of two, were busily engaged in cooking the eatables, arranging the tables, and putting things in order generally for the coming supper, and by the time the last load was "unpitched," the welcome announcement was made that all was ready. No second summons was needed, and in a very short time the carters, farm servants, and labourers, with faces glowing with expectation, and ruddy from a recent swill, arranged themselves round a long table; "meyaster" and his select circle, the carpenter and blacksmith generally included, being seated at a cross table at the top of the other, or if crowded, at a separate board, as near the labourers' table as convenient.

A large leg of mutton, a ham to match, or sometimes two; with mutton pies, or a chine, constituted the first course; followed by plum puddings of huge dimensions, sometimes accompanied by an apple pie of still larger diameter. "Meyaster" generally carved at the top of the table, and one of the invited guests at the bottom. All these dishes having been considerably lightened, and the table cleared,—"*Mensæque remotæ, crateras magnos statuunt et vina coronant.*" Jugs of real "Hooam Harvest Stingo," with pipes and tobacco, were placed before the men; and pipes and tobacco, with bottles of spirits, and the necessary ingredients for making grog, before "meyaster" and his party at the head of the table. Then one of the men was called upon for a song, and the business of the evening proceeded in the following fashion:—" Come Joe, open the ball, lets hay a zong." "I don't think I knows ar one, mayet." "I knows better than that, vor I've zid thee learnen one for the last dree weeks." "Well, what o' that? I dunno nor one all droo; and if I ded, I never was noo zinger." "Now then Joe, shet up! I've heerd ye rattle out '*I'm zebenteen come Zunday,*' proper, many's a time, zo let's hay it." "Well, if I most, I most, but I can't mind it all, I tell'ee." Joe, after a few vigorous hems, and a deep draught of ale, commences, in a tone in which strength made up for want of harmony :

"As I walked out one Maay mornen,
One Maay mornen so early,
I overtook a handsome maade,
Just as the zun was a risen.
Wi' my rum tum ta,
And my rum tum ta,
Fol lol the diddle lol the dido.

Now then come in coalbox [chorus] all zides,—ye don't half help a feller out. [Chorus repeated most vociferously.]

Her stockens white, her shoes was bright,
The buckles shined like zilver,
She had a black and a rollen eye,
And her hear hung down her showlders.
Wi' my rum tum ta, &c.

' How wold be you my pretty maade ?
How wold be you my honey ?'
She answered me right cheerfully,
' I'm zebenteen come Zunday.'
Wi' my rum tum ta, &c.

' Where be you gwyne my pretty maade ?
Where be you gwyne my honey ?'
She answered me right cheerfully,
' On a arrant vor my mammy.'
Wi' my rum tum ta, &c.

Ah, there's a hole in the ballet, I can't mind no more on't; but there's two or dree more verses I used to know one time." "I knows there es, Joe; this is a bit o' the taail end on't :

' If you will come to my mammy's house,
When the moon shines bright and clearly,'—

I know this vrom hearen Joe zing it several years agoo." "That's right, mayet, it comes in zomewhere, but I can't mind the rest on't, 'tes zo long agoo I zung it, 'tes all in a midgemadge wi' me now; so jest come in coalbox once moore, and let's finish it,—

Wi' my rum tum ta, &c.

Now Varmer Ben, I hope, zur, you'll gee us one o' yourn now aater me, and I knows you can zing a good one or two."

"No, no, Joe, I bean't up to consart pitch it; I'll come in vurder on, bimeby."

The oldest labourer on the farm, rising with deliberation: "Stop a bit, wullee, Joe, 'tes my turn now, and I ought to a ben avore you; I ben here on the plaace over twenty year, and I ben at all the Hooam Harvests but two all they years, and the vust thing that we used to do aater the taable was clear, when things was done in wold fashion style, was to drink meyaster's good health, all stannen up; so now vill your glasses, and I'll lead off." All stand up and join in the singing:

> "Here's a health unto our meyaster,
> The founder o' the feeast,
> I hopes wi' all my heart, bwoys,
> His soul in heaven med rest,
> That all the things wull prosper
> That ever he takes in hand,
> Vor we be all his sarvants,
> And all at his command.
> Then drink, boys, drink, and zee you do not spill,
> Vor if you do, you sholl drink two,
> If 'tes our meyaster's will."

"Hip, hip, hurrah," three times repeated, the last loudest. "One moore for missus."* "Now keerter, let's hay your ditty; you knows a good one or two, I be sure." "Well you, I do know one, what I picked up when I was a bwoy, by hearen my wold granny zingen on 'en; but I never rayly learned one, 'cause I can't rade." "Ah, Keerter, there was no National Schools about when we was bwoys." "Noa there wudden't, but I went to a night school, I minds, dree times one winter, after I come hooam from work; but the vust two times the schoolmeyaster dedn't show at all, and t'other time, when a ded, we hadn't got no candle, zo I dedn't larn but very little, and never was nothen of a schollard. However, here's my wold song—'Lumps o' Pudden':†

> When I lived at hooam as a bwoy,
> I was my mother's onny joy;
> You never would b'leeve, unless you did zee,
> What lumps o' pudden my mother gid me.
> Lumps o' pudden and dollops o' fat,
> My mother gid me to cock up my hat.

One day we killed a gurt fat pig,
And hung 'en up by the hinder lig;
She made black puddens as big as my knee,
And lumps o' pudden my mother gid me.
    Lumps o' pudden, &c.

The puddens was all hung up on a pin,
The fat run out and the hoppers got in;
I shall never vorgit, wherever I be,
What lumps o' pudden my mother gid me.
    Lumps o' pudden, &c.

She'd rout me up in the morn and zay
' Git up, my bwoy, without delay,
There's liver and pudden and sowse for thee,'
And lumps o' pudden my mother gid me.
    Lumps o' pudden, &c.

And at night, avore I went to bed,
She'd take out a pudden as big as my head;
I got zo fat I could hardly zee,
With the lumps o' pudden my mother gid me.
    Lumps o' pudden, &c."

"Haw, haw, haw. Well done keerter, that *es* a good wold zong; but you've lost a good deal o' your fat zunce you yet sich a lot o' pudden." "That I have you. I've worked hard in my time, but I bean't quite skin and booan it." "You knows wold Tom Buckett's son, don't ye,—that long zided, lanky feller, that goos by the neyam of 'Boxer'?" "Oi, I knows 'en very well; I should think a vew lumps of pudden would doo'n good by the look on 'en." "Well you, I met 'en just avore last Middlemas, t'other side of Idlecombe, stuck up on a geat by the zide o' the road, and looken like a bag o' booans; zo I zays to'n : 'Thee doesn't look very thriven, Boxer; I don't think the zun wull vetch much fat out on thee.' 'Noa, Harry,' a zed, ' I han't got much fat to lose jest now, but I be gwyne to live at Varmer Bull's, in house, at Middlemas, and there's plenty of good fat pork and hard pudden, and sich things there; and Lord zend! won't I yet and scoggil! I won't vill myself up wi' callards, I warn't it.' " (Roars of laughter.) "Now Jan White, come along, let's hay your favourite,—the wold harvest zong ; I heerd ye zing 'en two years agoo now, don't ye mind, at the Hooam Harvest over at Ducksmoor." " All right, Mister Read, and

I don't think I've zung 'en all droo zunce then; but let's wet my whistle, and I'll zee what I can do.

> Come all you jolly harvest men,
>   And listen vor a while;
> The zong that I be gwyne to zing,
>   Wull cause you all to smile.
>   And to harvest we wull go,
>   We wull go, we wull go.
>
> The corn is ripe, and fit to cut,
>   Our meyaster thought it right
> To employ we as harvest men,
>   Zo we be here to night.
>   And to harvest we wull go, &c.
>
> The lark, wi' his tuneful notes,
>   Begins the labouren day;
> Our meyaster calls us vrom our beds,
>   His call we most obey.
>   And to harvest we wull go, &c.
>
> We gapes awhile, and rubs our eyes,
>   To bread and cheese zets down,
> And ates a bit, and drinks a sup,
>   Our drowsiness to drown.
>   And to harvest we wull go, &c.
>
> We zets, and yets, and tipples,
>   Our meyaster stands behind,
> And gees us orders what to do,
>   Accorden to his mind.
>   And to harvest we wull go, &c.
>
> We then gits up, and takes our hats
>   And hooks, and march away;
> And labours on to breakfast time,
>   Without the laste delay.
>   And to harvest we wull go, &c.
>
> The puncheons bein empty,
>   And breakfast bein o'er,
> We look out then vor lebben o'clock,
>   When we sholl hay zome moore.
>   And to harvest we wull go, &c.
>
> So on we labours droo the day,
>   And toils on in the heat;
> Our meyaster zends unto the field
>   A plenteous store o' meeat.
>   And to harvest we wull go, &c.
>
> Wi' gearden stuff and pudden too
>   Our platters do abound;

    Wi' long clap knives and wooden forks
      We plaay a smurtish round.
            And to harvest we wull go, &c.
    We often whets our rip hooks,
      And looks up to the zun,
    And often wishes in ourzelves,
      The taydious work was done.
            And to harvest we wull go, &c.
    But nammet time revives our souls,
      Our droopen spirits cheers,
    Vor we begins to stast, and wants
      Zome good stiff nammet beer.
            And to harvest we wull go, &c.
    At vower o'clock, or thereabouts,
      Our nammet time arrives;
    We twigs the bwoy that brings it out,—
      That zets us all alive.
            And to harvest we wull go, &c.
    At zix o'clock, or thereabouts,
      We cracks our jokes and laughs;
    And zays one to another,
      ' Here comes zome half-and-half.'
            And to harvest we wull go, &c.
    At eight o'clock, or thereabouts,
      Our supper doth prevail;
    Bread and cheese, and good fat pork,
      Bezides a pint o' ale.
            And to harvest we wull go, &c.
    And now the harvest month is o'er,
      Until another year;
    And then if our meyaster plaize, agen
      We wull flog his beef and beer.
            And to harvest we wull go, &c."

"Well done, Jan, ye got droo wi' et vust ract; I never heerd ye zing it better." " 'Tes a good wold zong, and I should like to know'n myzelf; but I gid up zingen when tunes come into fashion." " Well Tom, I never heerd thee try to zing but once, and then I thought it sounded like the scroopen o' our waggon wheels when they wants gracen." "Well gennelmen, I bleeves I be 'titled to a call now; so Varmer Ben, we shall be glad if you'll gee us a little harmony." "Ah, I spooase I most Jan, vor I can zee 1 shan't hay no peace till I do; but what sholl it be?" " Oh, let's hay ' Will the Wayver,' varmer, that's the one; 'tes a good tune, and I never heerd anybody else zing it but you." Farmer Ben lays down his pipe, takes a good swig at his grog, leans back in his chair, and begins " Will the Weaver."

" ' Oh mother, mother, I be married,
Oh that I had longer tarried,
Vor the women do declare,
That the breeches they will wear.'

' Loven son, what es the matter?
Do she frown, or do she flatter?
Every time she do rebel,
Take a stick and twank her well.'

As he went hooam, a neighbour met him,
Jest the while that he was fretten.
Zays he : ' Young man, I'll tell ye who
It was that I zid wi' thy wife jest now.

There was thy wife, and Will the Wayver,
Oh, so loven, close together;
I zid them boath,—I'll zay no moore,
They went in doors, and shet the door.'

Then he went hooam, all in a wonder,
Rappen at the door like thunder;
' Who is there?' the wayver cried.
' Oh! 'tes my husband, and you most hide.'

Then up the chimbley quick he ventured,
And in the door her husband entered;
He searched the house and corners round,
And not a soul could there be vound.

Awhile he stood like one amazéd,
Then he up the chimbley gazéd;
There he spied the wretched soul,
Perched astride the cotterel pole.

' I be glad that I have vound thee,
I won't hang thee, nor I won't drown thee,
But I wull stufle thee wi' smoke ':
This he thought, but nothen spoke.

Then he knocked up a roaren vire,
For to plaise his own desire;
His wife cried out : ' My dearest Will !
Oh, husband ! oh, husband ! the man you'll kill!

' Take him down my dearest jewel,'
He kept heapen on moore fuel;
' Oh take him down, and spare his life,
And I wull be thy faithful wife.'

> Then off the cotterel pole he took him,
> And sever*ely* he shook him,
> And zed to him at every stroke,
> 'Come no moore to stop my smoke.'
> There was never nor poor chimbley sweeper
> Half so black as Will the Wayver,
> Hands and faace, and clothes likewise,
> And sent off hooam wi' two black eyes."

(Roars of laughter and applause.) "Brayvo varmer! that's the best zong we've had it." "I thought 'twould suit ye Jan; and to keep up the ball, I'll call upon Thomas there vor a zong." "A very good call, varmer; zo clear your pipes Thomas my wold hearty, and lets hay 'Whistle, daughter.'" "Noa, I dunno; 'tes onny a paacel o' wold foolishness, and ye can't come in coalbox nother." Come, come, Thomas, noo slippen out on't; moost on us never heerd *you* zing, zo lay back your years and spet it out proper." "I never could zing, mayet, but I have maade a hollobulloo avore now." Thomas, after several hems, and a deep draught of ale, shuts his eyes, and in a strident tone begins:

> "'Whistle, daughter, whistle, come whistle now my dear.'
> 'I cannot whistle, mammy, 'tes the wrong time o' the year.'
> 'Whistle, daughter, whistle, and you sholl hay a pound.'
> 'I cannot whistle, mammy, I cannot make a sound.'
> 'Whistle, daughter, whistle, and you sholl hay a cow.'
> 'I cannot whistle, mammy, I rayly don't know how.'
> 'Whistle, daughter, whistle, and you sholl hay a man.'
> 'I cannot whistle, mammy, but I'll do the best I can.'"

"Haw, haw, haw; well done Thomas, we dedn't know you was sich a zinger avore; well done our zide." "Oi, Thomas's zong was like a jackass's gallop, short and sweet." "Well, 'tes the onny ditty I knows, and the shorter 'tes, the zooner its over; zo I'll light my pipe, and jest call on Mr. Cooper vor the next zong, 'cause I knows he's a good zinger, and zo was his father avore'n." "Very well, Thomas, you sholl have a sporting ditty this time, and I louz that'll suit ye."

THE JOVIAL SPORTSMEN.

> There was zome jolly sportsmen
> Went out to hunt a fox,

And where d'ye think they vound him?
  Among the hills and rocks.
With my whoop, whoop, whoop, and my halloa!
All in this merry train;
With my ran, tan, tan, and my tivy, tivy, twang;
Right droo the woods we'll ride, brave bwoys,
Right droo the woods we'll ride.

  The vust we met was a ploughman,
    A ploughen of his land;
  He swore he zid bold Renyard
    Run by on his right hand.
      With my whoop, whoop, whoop, &c.

  The next we met was a miller,
    A peepen out o' his mill;
  He swore he zid bold Renyard
    Run up the yonder hill.
      With my whoop, whoop, whoop, &c.

  The next we met was a blind man,
    As blind as he could be;
  He swore he zid bold Renyard
    Run up a hollow tree.
      With my whoop, whoop, whoop, &c.

  The next we met was a paason,
    Clad in his mournen black;
  He swore he zid bold Renyard
    Run up the huntsman's back.
      With my whoop, whoop, whoop, &c."

"Well done, Mr. Cooper, yourn es zummet like a zong,—plenty of coalbox in 'en." "Thankee, Mr. Cooper, 'tes

  A very good zong, and very well zung,
  Jolly companions every one."

"Oi you, I heerd wold Tom Chiverton's son try to zing that zong in at the Rid Lion jest aater last harvest, but a couldn't make half a job on't." "I was there, you; 'twas middle Bargain Zadderday, and I run up agen 'en in Beeast Market, avore a got into the Red Lion. 'Hollo, mayet,' I zays, 'where'st thee spring vrom? where bist livin now, you?' ''Tes never you, Ned,' a zed, 'es it? Why I han't a zid thy wold physog ever zunce last year. However dost git on, you?' 'Oh I be all right zo fur,' I zays, 'but where bist liven then?' 'Well,' a zed, 'I *was* liven at Nettlecombe, but I be liven now wi' wold varmer Stakebittle, down Lower Latchetts.' 'Thee doesn't zay zo,' zays I, 'and whatever hast got to do there?' 'Oh I onny keeps the kay o' the vuz house, and draves the ducks to water.' 'Tell'ee what 'tes, mayet,' I zays, 'simmen to me thee hast got a good aisy plaace, and thee'st better look out and keep 'en. But what dost git a year?' 'Zix pound,' a zed, 'but nor nammet, you.' I thought I'd heerd quite enough wi' that, zo I wished 'en good day, and went a little vurder on." "Well men, time's on the wing, and there's Andrew there zetten all the evenen as mute as a mouse, but he can zing a good zong if a mind to." "Hear, hear, meyaster. Now Andrew, let's hay 'The little Cappender.'" Andrew deliberately fills his glass, empties it, and commences—

The Little Cappender.

"I'll zing you a new zong, that layetly has been maade,
'Tes of a little cappender, and of a pretty maade.
I have a fancy vor you, you goos zo neat and trim;
But oh, the little cappender, what wull become of him?

The vust was a varmer, and he could plough and zow;
He zed, 'My pretty fair maade, I'm come to let you know
I have a fancy vor you, you goos so neat and trim;
But oh, the little cappender, what wull become of him?'

The next was a wold man come hoppen in the dark;
He zed, 'My dearest jewel, 'tes you have won my heart;
I have a fancy vor you, you goos zo neat and trim;
But oh, the little cappender, what wull become of him?'

The next was a blacksmith that come vrom Newtown fair,
He gid her his goold watch, and a little of his store,
He gid her his silk handkercher all vor to putt it in,
Zaying, 'Oh, the little cappender, what wull become of him?'

'I'll work wi' my broad axe, as long as I can wag,
And all the money I can git, I'll putt it in the bag,
I'll putt it in my bag, until Zadderday at night,
And 'tes oh, my little cappender, you be my heart's delight.'"

"Well done Andrew, that's a rale good wold zong; I minds hearen my father zing 'en, years agoo." "Oi you, and I heerd wold Gladdis zing 'en in Nippert, one Bargain Zadderday one time. I zay Sam, wudden't thee there too?" "I jist about was, mayet; Sal and I was there, and we went up in Bell Chamber rish, and had dree pennorth o' rid stuff apiece, and a good step or two aaterwards; wold Keech was there wi' his fiddle, and another young chap to help, but he couldn't scraape it out like Keech." "Dedn't ye zee a ghost gwyne hooam that night, and all git uptipped in the road? I fancies I heerd zo at the time." "Haw, haw; zee a ghost! noa; we wudden't *quite* so zoat as that, but we did git auverdrowed, and the rine knocked off zome on us. You know you, jist as we was about starten hooamwards, we meets wi' wold Honey in his light keert, wi' that gurt chesnut mare o' hes, and a had 'Skiver ligs' and wold Whittul in the keert wi' 'en, and all on 'em was about half cocked. 'Come on Sam,' a zays, 'there's room vor thee and Sal,—jump up behind;' zo we ded, and there was a good looad on us, I can tell'ee. We got on very well till we was jest t'other zide o' Rookley, when all at once the wold mare shied at a wold gallybagger stuck up top o' hedge, and swealed round right athirt the road, and one of the wheels come off, and all the hool bwilen on us vell out wi' sich a louster right in the middle o' the road; we maade the mud vlee, I'll war'nt it. I went sprawlen in a gurt heap on't, and Sal right up top on me. Wudden't I in a mess, you! Honey, he vell athirt wold Whittul's geeam lig, and maade 'en zwear like a trooper. Skiver ligs had his head cut about, and lost his new hat; and I had a miserable black eye, and was zo tender all over vor a day or two aaterwards that I couldn't hardly wag. Wold Honey and Sal come off best,—they wudden't hurt; but Honey lost his whip, and Sal spwiled her head gear; zo I had to paay vor a new bonnet vor her the week aater." "Oi, you, I zid Skiver ligs the next day, and a was battered a bit about the pimple on 'en." "Humph, that was nothen; you ought to zee wold 'Pay shucks' zometimes, aater he and his wold do oman have had a pint or two, and a bit of a dido over night; the faace on 'en looks like a ground fresh ploughed, wi' a good many baaks left here and there." (Roars of laughter). "Well chaps, if we meeans to hay ar nother zong we must be sharp, vor the time's gitten on, and 'twull zoon be shet up time; zo come on Mister Morris, we han't had your ditty it, and you can gee us the best wold zong we've had to-night, I knows very well." "Ah, Mister Morris, jest let's hay 'Zed Jan to Joan.'" "Well, I thought I should hay to make a noise avore the night was over, zo I'll try what I can do to plaise ye.

§ Zed Jan to Joan, 'Wull you hay me?
  Vor if you wull, I'll marry thee.
  I've house, and land, and cows, and swine,
  And if you likes, it med all be thine.
    Then tell me Joan if this wull do,
    Vor I can't come every day to woo.

My barn wi' corn and haay is vull,
I've dreo fat pigs jest ready to kill,
I've got a mare which es coal black,
She'll car me well, and also a zack.
   Then tell me Joan, &c.

A good fat cheese lays on my shilf,
I never sholl yet it all myself,
And up the chimley, saafe in a nitch,
Es twenty guineas, 'long zide o' the flitch.
   Then tell me Joan, &c.

You zees o' wealth I got good stoore,—
When mother dies I sholl hay zome moore;
I've house, and land, and goold in puss,
You med goo vurder and fare wuss.
   Then tell me Joan, &c.

I hopes I sholl git your consent,
But I be noo hand at compliment,
I be moore at hooam in the ground at plough,
When I hollers—whup! and whoa! gee whoa!
   Then tell me Joan, &c.'"

"Bravo, well done, Mister Morris, that's about the best thing we've had to-night, simmen to me." "Hollo Andrew, thee begins to look goggle eyed; drink up, mayet, we must zoon begin to clear out." "I be right enough Jan; mind thee doesn't goo and vall into the hull coop to-night, as ye ded the Hooam Harvest avore last,—I minds it min." "Haw, haw, that was a pretty goo, Jan. But come, Thomas, can't you gee us a verse or two vor a finisher?" "Noa, I can't; I zung all I knowed a nower agoo, as I told ye, zo I be plaayed out." "Well, I can tell a little bit of a yarn about Thomas, that'll make ye laugh." "Can ye, Andrew? well, do let's hay it." "Zome years agoo, when Thomas used to run about wi' wold Cook's daughter—Sairey Ann, I thinks she was called,—I happened to be in the Rose and Crown one Nippert Fair day, when who should come in but Thomas and hes gal. 'Well Sairey Ann,' a zays, 'let's hay zummet. What be ye gwyne to hay you? Here missus, gimme dree pennorth o' that cre rid stuff out o' the bottle.' 'Oh Thomas,' zays Sairey, 'don't putt yourself to sich expense.' 'Darn expense,' zays Thomas, 'I don't keer a cuss about expense; gee her a ha-penny biscuit, and let me hay another dree pennorth myself.'" " Now thee'st better shet up, Andrew; I've had about enough o' that." " All right, Thomas; don't take noo notice o' he—he edden't right half hes time; but let's hay one moore zong." " Stop a bit ; why here's Sam,—he ben yopplen a good deal to-night, but a han't gid us nor zong ; a can do't if a likes." " Oi, that *es* right; we've overlooked you, Sam; you knows jest the zong to top up wi',—one wi' a coalbox where we can all come in and rare the ruff ; zo unbutton your shirt collar, and let's hay ' Tally ho, hark away.' " || " All right keerter, mind ye stricks in, in the proper plaace.

> The zun was jest a peepen up over the hill,
> The ploughboy was whistlen along 'cross the field,
> The blackbirds was a zingen all each on his spray;
> Zays the Huntsman to his hounds : ' Tally ho, hark away.'
>   Tally ho, hark away, Tally ho, hark away,
>   Tally ho, tally ho,
>   Tally ho, hark away.
>
> Come up, my braave sportsmen, and make no delay,
> Come zaddle your hosses, and let's brish away;
> Vor the fox he's in view, all kindled wi' scorn,
> Zoo come my braave sportsmen and jine the shrill horn.
>   Tally ho, hark away, &c.
>
> He led us in chase vull fifty long miles,
> Over hedges, over deetches, over geats, over stiles ;
> Zo come my braave huntsman, sound your musical horn,
> We shall zoon overtake'n, vor his brush drags along.
>   Tally ho, hark away, &c.
>
> He led us in chase vor zix hours in vull cry ;
> Tally ho, hark away, vor the fox he must die ;
> Then we'll cut off his brush with view holloas and noise,
> And we'll drink a good health to all fox hunten bwoys.
>   Tally ho, hark away, &c.

Now chaps, coalbox ! One moore vor a top up." (Chorus thrice repeated, fortissimo, and ended with unbounded applause.)

The labourers and farm servants then wished their master and his guests good night, and retired; " meyaster " and his party remaining for half-an-hour's chat over a last pipe and parting glass. The next day was always more or less a holiday, being the day following the feast, when nobody felt much disposed for sustained labour after the late hours and revelry of the preceding night; odd jobs were finished, and things generally put in order; the men engaged for the month were paid, and after a few jugs of foaming harvest beer had gone round, departed for their homes; in most cases taking to their wives and families some of the remnants of the harvest supper. The chief celebration of farming life was over for the year, and in this now disused merry-making much more genuine hospitality was practised, and more kindly feelings engendered, than in any number of Harvest Festivals as at present conducted. The farmer had taken part in the labours of his men, and often sat at the same table at dinner and supper with them during the harvest month, and at the closing joviality of "Hooam Harvest" delighted with his friends to mix with his men without constraint or distinction; thus forming a bond of union and sympathy between them and himself, of which in these days of freezing political economics, and subjection of everything to the rigid rule of supply and demand, we have scarcely any conception, and practically realising the honest and homely lines of old Tusser—

"In harvest time, harvest folk, servants and all,
Should make altogether good cheer in the hall,
And fill up the black bowl, so blithe to their song,
And let them be merrie all harvest time long.

Once ended thy harvest, let none be beguiled,
Please such as did please thee, man, woman, and child.
Thus doing, with alway such help as they can,
Thou winnest the praise of the labouring man."

NOTES.

* Sometimes, according to the knowledge of the singers, instead of an extra cheer for " Missus," an additional verse in her commendation was sung, as follows :—

" Now harvest it is over, and summer it is past,
  We'll drink our Missus's health in a full and flowing glass ;
  For she is a good woman, and gives us all good cheer,
  So come my brave boys, let's all tip off our beer.
        Then drink boys, drink, &c."

† " Lumps o' Pudden." A version of this song, but varying a good deal from that here given, with the tune, is in D'Urfey's " Pills to purge Melancholy."

‡ This very curious rustic song, now almost forgotten, is here printed it is believed for the first time, as also most of those following—" Will the Weaver," "The Little Cappender, &c."

§ " Zed Jan to Joan," better known as " The Clown's Courtship." This song, with the tune, is to be found in D'Urfey's " Pills to purge Melancholy," and also in Chappell's " Popular Music of the Olden Time." The version sung in the Isle of Wight differs a good deal from that given in either of these works, and having been modernised, has lost much of its quaintness; but it has an additional verse, wanting in each of the others. Mr. Chappell considers the song to be as old as the reign of Henry VIII., the first verse having been found set to music in a MS. of that date.

‖ " Tally ho, hark away." This is a favourite song among the peasantry, principally on account of its rollicking chorus, which can be repeated *ad lib.* Fox-hunting songs are not generally native productions, but importations from the mainland, dating from about the middle or end of the last century; as foxes were not introduced into the Island till after the year 1840.

SONGS SUNG BY THE PEASANTRY IN THE ISLAND.

The native songs of the Isle of Wight are not remarkable for their excellence, their range of expression is limited, and the romantic and chivalrous element found in the ballads and songs of other parts of England is almost wholly wanting. They may be roughly classed as: Amatory; Naval, generally with a mixture of amorous sentiment; Bucolic; and Humourous and Satirical. Many of the Amatory songs so closely resemble each other in subject and diction as to be almost monotonous; the hero walks abroad early in the morning "to take the air," meets with "some lovely fair," and after a pause for reflection, he screws his courage to the sticking point, "boldly steps up to her," and accosts her. The phrases quoted are however of considerable antiquity, and may be found in songs, from the end of the reign of Elizabeth to the close of the seventeenth century. Most of the naval songs are probably importations; many of Dibden's are still current, but these are too well known to be here inserted. Versions of many of the following songs are to be met with in other parts of the country; but a large proportion have been taken down from the lips of the singers, and it is believed now for the first time appear in print.

Abroad as I was Walking.

Abroad as I was walking,
  Down by a river side,
I heard a fair maid sing a song,
  And it caused me long to bide, to bide,
  And it caused me long to bide.

I boldly stepped up to her,
  And thanked her for her song,
Then asked her if she would marry me;
  But her answer was, "Too young, too young,
  But her anwer was, "Too young."

"The younger, my fair pretty maid,
　More fitting for my bride;
That I may say some other day,
　I married my wife a maid, a maid,
　I married my wife a maid."
Then we sat down together,
　Till day did disappear;
Then up she rose, and shook her clothes,
　And sang, "Fare you well my dear, my dear,
　And sang, "Fare you well, my dear."
"There's a plant grows in my garden,
　And some do call it thyme;
So you may dance with your true love,
　And I will dance with mine, with mine,
　And I will dance with mine."

THE MAIDEN'S COMPLAINT.

I walked abroad one morning,
　All in the month of May,
To hear the small birds whistle,
　And to see the young lambs play;
I overheard young Susan,
　Her voice was low and clear—
"Long time have I been waiting
　For the coming of my dear."

I drew myself beside a tree,
　With branches broad and green,
The leaves they overshaded me,
　So I could not be seen;
I sat me down and listened,
　While she began to moan—
"Ah! woeful me, and sad the day;
　My heart is not my own.

My mind is sad and troubled,
　Sometimes I think I'll go
Unto my heedless true love,
　And all my passion show;
And yet if I should do so,
　I fear 'twould be in vain,—
I'd show to him my boldness,
　He'd ne'er love me again.

I cannot think the reason
　Why women love young men,
For they are so falsehearted,
　And true not one in ten;

It's always their endeavour
Young women to trepan;
So the green grave shall cover me,
Before I'll trust a man."

THE BANKS OF THE SWEET PRIMROSES.

As I walked out one Midsummer morning
To view the fields and to take the air,
Down by the banks of the sweet primroses,
There I beheld a most lovely fair.
'Twas three long steps I took up to her,
Not knowing her as she passed me by;
I stepped up to her, thinking to view her,
She seemed to me like some virtuous bride.
Said I "Fair maid, where are you going?
And what is the reason of all your grief?
I will make you as happy as any lady,
If you will let me give you relief."
"Stand off! stand off! you are deceivers,
You are a false and deluding man;
'Twas you that caused my poor heart to wander,
And to give me comfort is all in vain.
I will go down in some lonesome valley,
Where no man on earth shall there me find,
Where the pretty little small birds do hush their voices;
And drown my sighs in the blustering wind."

THE SPOTTED COW.

One morning in the month of May,
As from my cot I strayed,
Just at the dawning of the day,
I met a charming maid.
" Good morning; whither my fair maid
So early, tell me now?"
The maid replied, " Good sir," she said,
" I've lost my spotted cow."
" Do not complain," to her I said,
" Your cow's not lost, my dear,
I saw her down in yonder mead;
Come love—I'll show you where,'

" I must confess that you are kind;
    I thank you, sir," said she.
" You will be sure your cow to find,
    Come sweetheart, go with me."

Then to the fields we did repair,
    Down in the flowery vale;
We hugged and kissed each other there,
    And love was all our tale.

And in the groves we spent the day,
    And thought it passed too soon;
At night we homewards bent our way,
    When brightly shone the moon.

And should I cross that flowery vale,
    Or go to drive the plough,
She comes and calls, " My gentle swain,
    I've lost my spotted cow."

CUPID'S GARDEN.

The tune of this favourite song is given in Chappell's Popular Music, and is the same as sung in the Island. The copy given of the words, in four stanzas, is also nearly identical; except the last, which is very different, and much inferior to the Island version. According to Dr. Rimbault, "Cupid's Garden" is a corruption of "Cuper's Gardens," a noted place of amusement on the Surrey side of the Thames, opposite Somerset House. They were opened in 1678, and for a long time maintained their celebrity, being laid out in walks decorated with statuary, with convenient arbours for retirement. The gardens were also famous for displays of fireworks; but being superseded by the superior attractions of Vauxhall, were finally closed in 1753.

'Twas down in Cupid's garden
    For pleasure I did go,
To view the fairest flowers
    That in that garden grow;
The first it was the jessamine,
    The lily, pink, and rose;
They are the fairest flowers
    That in that garden grows.

I had not walked in that garden
    The best part of an hour,
When I did spy two pretty maids
    Sitting in a shady bower;
The first was lovely Nancy,
    So beautiful and fair;
The other was a virgin,
    Who did the laurel wear.

I boldly stepped up to her,
  And unto her did say—
"Are you engaged to any young man?
  Come tell me now, I pray."
"I'm not engaged to any young man,
  I solemnly declare;
I mean to live a virgin,
  And still the laurel wear."

"Well then," said I unto her,
  "If that's your firm intent,
I'll give my hand to Nancy,
  If I have her consent."
We both walked off together,
  Saying, "Wear your laurel still,
For she that will not when she may,
  She shall not when she will."

THE GARDENER'S CHOICE.

This curious old song is a general favourite; the tune and the words are to be found in Chappell's Popular Music. A somewhat different version of the words is also in Bell's Songs and Ballads of the Peasantry of England. According to Dr. Whitaker, the original song was written by Mrs. Fleetwood Habergham, of the County of Lancashire, who died in 1703, disappointed and ruined by the vices of her husband. All versions of the song appear to be more or less corrupt, and that here given is quite different in many places from those printed by Chappell and Bell, by whom the song is entitled, "The Seeds of Love."

It was in the Merry Month of May
  When the sun begins for to shine;
I had three branches all for to choose one,
  And the one that I chose was thyme.

Oh, thyme it is the most precious root
  That ever the sun shone on;
For time will bring all things to an end,
  And so our time runs on.

The gardener, he was standing by,
  I asked him to choose for me;
He chose me the violet, the lily, and the pink,
  But those flowers I refused all three.

The violet I refused at once,
  Because it fades so soon;
The lily and the pink I also overlooked,
  And resolved I would tarry to June.

In June there is a red rosy bud,
    And that's the flower for me ;
And often have I thought on that red rosy bud,
    Which has gained me the willow, willow tree.

Oh, the willow, the willow, it will twist,
    And the willow tree it will twine ;
And I wish I was in that dear youth's arms
    That stole away my sprig of thyme.

The gardener he was standing by,
    And he told me to take care ;
For in the middle of that red rosy bud,
    A very sharp thorn grows there.

Some venomous thorn grows there I know,
    For yet I feel the smart ;
And the thorn underneath that red rosy bud
    Has pierced my tender heart.

" Stand up, stand up," to my heart said I,
    " And still to thyself prove true ;
Though my garden that once was covered with thyme,
    Is now overgrown with rue."

Roger and Dolly.

Once down in our village lived a parson and his wife,
Who led a very decent kind of comfortable life ;
They kept a serving man and maid, as neat as neat could be,
The maid was fond of Roger, and Roger fond of she.

The parson's wife kept Dolly so very close to work,
She might as well been servant to a Dutchman or a Turk ;
But though she was employed all day, as busy as a bee,
She only thought of Roger, and Roger thought of she.

The parson was an old man, but would have done amiss,
For he got her in a corner, and asked her for a kiss ;
But Dolly quickly let him know, as plain as plain could be,
She only wanted Roger, and Roger wanted she.

By love and work together, this maid fell very ill,
The doctor soon was sent for, and tried his utmost skill ;
She wouldn't take his physic, though bad as bad could be,—
She only wanted Roger, and Roger wanted she.

But when the parson found 'twas love only made her bad,
He very kindly said, " She had better have the lad ";
The sight of Roger made her well, as well as she could be ;
They married—she had Roger, and Roger he had she.

RICHARD OF TAUNTON DEAN.

This song is popular with the country people in various parts of England, particularly in the south-western counties. Versions of it are to be found in Chappell's Popular Music, and in Bell's Songs of the Peasantry; but that here given varies in several places from either of them.

Last New Year's Day, as I've heard say,
Young Richard he mounted his dapple grey;
Away he rode to Taunton Dean,
To court the parson's daughter Jean.
  Fal a la la, fal a la la,
  Right too tooral, fal a la la.

His buckskin breeches he put on,
His gooseberry coat and clouted shoon,
Likewise his hat upon his head
Was trimmed all round with ribbons red.
  Fal a la la, &c.

Thus Richard he rode along in state,
Until he came to the parson's gate,
Where he knocked and shouted and cried "Holloa!
Be the folks at home? say yes or no."
  Fal a la la, &c.

A trusty old servant soon let him in,
That Richard his courtship might begin;
He stamped and strutted about the hall,
And loud for Mistress Jean did call.
  Fal a la la, &c.

So Mistress Jean came down straightway,
To hear what Richard had got to say;
" Why, doesn't thee know me Mistress Jean?
I be honest Dick of Taunton Dean.
  Fal a la la, &c.

My mother she sent me here to woo,
And I can fancy none but you;
So if you loves me as I loves you,
What signifies so much to do."
  Fal a la la, &c.

" If I consent to be your bride,
What living for me can you provide?
For I can neither card nor spin,
Churn butter, nor help bring harvest in."
  Fal a la la, &c.

" Why I can plough, and I can sow,
And sometimes to the market go,

> With old Dame Dobson's cartload of hay,
> I can earn my sixpence every day."
> > Fal a la la, &c.
>
> " But sixpence a day will never do,
> For I must have silks and satins too;
> Besides a fine coach to ride out in the air."
> " Oh, dang it," says Dick, " thee makes me swear."
> > Fal a la la, &c.
>
> " But I have a house that stands hard by,
> 'Twill be all my own when mother do die;
> And if you'll consent to marry me now,
> I'll make ye as fat as my mother's old sow."
> > Fal a la la, &c.
>
> Thus Dick, with his compliments so polite,
> Made all the family laugh outright;
> Which he took so in anger, no longer he'd stay,
> So he mounted his dapple and rode away.
> > Fal a la la, &c.

Cis and Harry.

This song, which is probably as ancient as the reign of Charles II., is to be found in D'Urfey's "Pills." The version there given is considerably longer, and except the first stanza, different, besides being grossly indelicate.

> The clock had struck, but I can't tell ye what,
> And the morning looked as grey as a rat;
> Cocks and hens from their roosts did fly,
> Grunting pigs had left their stye,
> Down in the vale--Cis with her pail,
> There she met with her true lover Harry;
> First they kissed, and then shook fists,
> And talked like two fools just about to marry.
>
> " Od zooks!" said Hal, " I can't but think,
> Now we be come to wedlock's brink,
> What a fine breed one day 'twill be,
> That will be got 'twixt you and me."
> Cis at this gave him a kiss,
> Hugged him as if she'd burn him to tinder.
> Thus they woo, till Cis cried, " Phoo!
> There's my mistress looking out o' winder."
>
> Away Cis started without more ado,
> Harry stared a moment, and then he ran too;
> But he didn't overtake her for nearly a mile,
> Just as she came to a three-barred stile.

There Cis slipped—over heels she tripped,
Harry nearly split his sides with laughter;
What made him so—I don't know;
But they were married the next Monday after.

THE OLD MAN CLOTHED IN LEATHER.

Is apparently an abridgment of a song published in D'Urfey's "Pills," and is at least as old as the time of Charles I. The tune, and a specimen of the words, are in Chappell's Popular Music.

'Twas on a misty morning,
  And cloudy was the weather,
I met with an old man
  Who was clothéd all in leather;
He had no shirt unto his back,
  But wool unto his skin;
    With how do you do? and how do you do?
    And how do you do agen?

This old man was a thresher,
  His flail he daily plied;
He had a leather bottle
  He carried by his side,
And with a cap of lambswool
  He covered cheek and chin;
    With how do you do? &c.

I went a little further,
  And there I met a maid,
A going then a milking,
  "A milking, sir," she said;
Then I began to flatter her,
  And she began to sing;
    With how do you do? &c.

This maid her name was Dolly,
  She wore a gown of grey;
I being somewhat jolly,
  Prevailed on her to stay;
Then straight I fell to courting her,
  In hope her love to win;
    With how do you do? &c.

I told her I would marry,
  And she should be my bride;
That long I should not tarry,
  And twenty things beside;
That I would plough, and reap, and mow,
  While she could sit and spin;
    With how do you do? &c.

"Kind sir, I have a father,
    A mother too," said she;
"And truly I would rather
    They should decide for me;
For if I were undutiful
    To them 'twould be a sin";
        With how do you do? &c.

Away we quickly trudged it,
    And to her parents went;
And when we both got thither,
    I asked for their consent.
"You seem an honest man, sir,
    I pray you to come in";
        With how do you do? &c.

As Dolly she was willing,
    Her parents soon agreed;
They gave her forty shilling,
    We married were with speed;
And Dick the fiddler he did play,
    And all did dance and sing;
        With how do you do? and how do you do?
    And how do you do agen?

THE BANKS OF THE SWEET DUNDEE.

The word "Dundee" in the Island is always pronounced "*Dandee.*" The song is a favourite at rural festivities.

It's of a farmer's daughter, so beautiful I'm told,
Her parents died and left her five hundred pounds in gold;
She livéd with her uncle—the cause of all her woe,
And you soon shall hear this maiden fair did prove his overthrow.

Her uncle had a ploughboy, young Mary loved full well,
And in her uncle's garden their tales of love would tell;
There was a wealthy squire, who oft came her to see,
But still she loved her ploughboy on the banks of the sweet Dundee.

It was a summer morning—her uncle went straightway,
And knockéd at her bedroom door, and thus to her did say:
"Come, rise up pretty maiden, a lady you may be;
The squire is waiting for you on the banks of the sweet Dundee."

"A fig for all your squires, your lords, and dukes likewise;
My William's love appears to me like diamonds in my eyes."
"Begone, unruly maiden, you ne'er shall happy be,
For I will banish William from the banks of the sweet Dundee."

Her uncle and the squire rode out that summer day;
"Young William is in favour," her uncle he did say;
"But 'tis my firm intention to tie him to a tree,
    Or else to bribe the pressgang on the banks of the sweet Dundee."

The pressgang came to William, when he was all alone;
He boldly fought for liberty, but they were six to one;
The blood did flow in torrents; "Come kill me now," said he,
"I would rather die for Mary on the banks of the sweet Dundee."

This maid one day was walking, lamenting for her love,
When she met the wealthy squire down in her uncle's grove;
He clasped his arms around her—"Stand off, base wretch!" said she,
"You sent the only lad I love from the banks of the sweet Dundee."

He clasped his arms around her, and tried to throw her down,—
Two pistols and a sword she spied beneath his velvet gown;
Young Mary seized the weapons, his sword he used so free,
But she did fire, and shot the squire, on the banks of the sweet Dundee.

Her uncle, waiting, heard the noise, and hastened to the ground:
"Since you have killed the squire," said he, "I'll give you your death wound."
"Stand off! stand off!" said Mary, "undaunted I will be."
She the trigger drew, and her uncle slew, on the banks of the sweet Dundee.

The doctor then was sent for,—a man of noted skill,
Likewise there came the lawyer, for him to make his will.
He willed his gold to Mary, who fought so manfully;
Then closed his eyes, no more to rise, on the banks of the sweet Dundee.

About a twelvemonth after, or perhaps a little more,
The fleet returned to England, and William came ashore;
He hastened to his Mary, and who so glad as she?
They soon were wed, and happy lived, on the banks of the sweet Dundee.

I'M IN HASTE.

As 'cross the fields the other morn
    I tripped so blithe and gay,
The squire with his dog and gun,
    By chance came by that way.
"Whither so fast, sweet maid?" he cried,
    And caught me round the waist;
"Pray stop awhile." "Good sir," said I,
    "I can't, for I'm in haste."

"You must not go as yet," said he,
   "For I have much to say;
Come now sit down, and let us chat,
   Upon this new made hay.
I've loved you long, and oft have wished
   Those ruby lips to taste;
I'll have a kiss."   "Well then," said I,
   "You can't, for I'm in haste."

Just as I spoke, I saw young Hodge
   Come through a neighbouring gate;
He took my hand and said, "Dear girl,
   I fear I've made you wait;
But here's the ring, come let's to church,
   The joys of love to taste."
I left the squire, and laughing cried,
   "You see, sir, I'm in haste."

THE DARK-EYED SAILOR.

It's of a handsome young lady fair,
Was walking out for to take the air;
She met a sailor upon her way,
So I paid attention to what she did say.

The sailor said, "Why roam alone?
The night is coming and the day near gone."
She cried, while tears from her eyes did fall,—
"It's a dark-eyed sailor that will be my downfall.

It's two long years since he left the land,
I took a gold ring from off my hand;
We broke the token—here's a part with me,
And the other's rolling at the bottom of the sea."

He answered, "Drive him from your mind,
Some other sailor as good you'll find;
Love turns aside and soon cold does grow,
As a winter morning when fields are clothed with snow."

These words did Phœbe's sad heart inflame;
Said she, "On me you shall play no game;"
She drew a dagger, and then did cry,
"For my dark-eyed sailor I lived and I will die.

His coal-black eye, and his curling hair,
And pleasant tongue, did my heart ensnare;
Genteel he was—and no rake like you,
To advise a maiden to slight the jacket blue.

But still," said Phœbe, " I will ne'er disdain
A tarry sailor, but will treat the same;
So drink his health—here's a piece of coin,*
But my dark-eyed sailor still claims this heart of mine."
Then half the ring did young William show,—
She seemed distracted between joy and woe.
" Oh, welcome William, I have lands and gold
For my dark-eyed sailor, so handsome, true, and bold."
Then in a village down by the sea,
They joined in wedlock, and well agree.
All maids be true when your love's away,—
A cloudy morning oft brings a shining day.

The Sailor's Return.

A song on a very similar subject to the preceding, with the addition of local colouring.

'Twas on a wintry evening, the weather it was wet,
Upon the slope of Portsdown hill a damsel there I met;
I overheard her wailing, and sorrowing complain,
All for her absent sailor who ploughed the raging main.

I stepped up to the damsel, and put her in surprise,
I saw she did not know me—I being in disguise;
Said I, " My charming creature, my joy and heart's delight,
Wherever are you travelling this dark and stormy night?"

" The road, kind sir, to Portsmouth, if you will kindly show,
Unto a maid distracted,—for there I want to go;
I am searching for a young man, and Johnny is his name,
And in the fleet at Portsmouth I am told he does remain.

If he was here this night, he would shield me from all harm;
But he is on the ocean in his naval uniform,
And with brave Admiral Hawke he will all his foes destroy,
Like the roving kings of honour, who fought in the wars of Troy."

" It is six weeks or better since your true love left the shore,—
He's cruising on the ocean where the raging billows roar;
He went to sail the ocean for honour and for gain,
But I hear that he was shipwrecked upon the coast of Spain."

When she heard this dreadful news she fell into despair,
She fell to wringing of her hands and tearing of her hair:
" Since he is gone and left me, no man on earth I'll take,
But in some lonely valley I will wander for his sake."

* Pronounced *qieyne*,

My heart was full,—her anguish no longer could I see;
I clasped her in my arms, and said, "Look Jenny, look at me!
I am your faithful Johnny, I am neither drowned nor slain!
And now we've met so happily, we'll never part again."

THE PRETTY PLOUGHBOY.

It's of a pretty ploughboy who was driving of his team,
    And a fair pretty maid he did spy;
He unto her did say, " At home you'd better stay,"
    And away he went singing to his plough.

And this was his song as he trudged on his way,—
    " Pretty maid, you are of high degree;
If you should fall in love, and your parents not approve,
    The next thing they will send me off to sea."

As soon as this her cruel parents came to know,
    And he was a ploughing on a hill,
To him the pressgang came, and they sent him o'er the main,
    And he's gone in the wars to be slain.

But his love dressed herself in a man's suit of clothes,
    And she went for her ploughboy to search,
With her pockets lined with gold—she met a sailor bold,
    And these words unto her he did say—

" Where are you a going, my fair pretty maid,
    So anxious and so early in the morn?"
" They have pressed my love," said she, " and have sent him to sea,
    And he's gone in the wars to be slain!"

Said he, " My pretty maid, will you go along with me?"
    And she went with the sailor to his boat;
So they pushed from the shore, while the cannons they did roar,
    Which caused her to shed many tears.

So he rowed her along till they came to the ship,
    On board which her pretty ploughboy sailed;
" He is here," the captain said, " you are welcome pretty maid;
    But he's going in the wars to be slain."

But a hundred bright guineas at once she put down,
    And the captain he soon told them o'er;
" Now you for him have paid, you can take him, pretty maid,"
    And she hugged him till she got him safe ashore.

So all you pretty fair maids, wherever you may be,
    That values your true love more than gold;
You must cross the raging main, and fetch him back again,
    And I'll warrant you'll be happy till you die.

THE LOST SAILOR.

A very similar song to that preceding, but with a different termination. They both give a glimpse of a bygone state of society, and are general favourites at Harvest and Christmas time.

'Tis of an old miser who in London did dwell,—
He had but one daughter, whom a sailor loved well;
And when the old miser was out of the way,
She was always with her sailor by night and by day.

Soon as the old miser he heard of the news,
Straightway to the captain he immediately goes,
Crying—" Captain, bold captain, I have good news to tell,
I have got a young sailor for a bargain to sell—

So what you give me ?" this old man did say.
" I'll give you ten guineas, and take him away;
I'll send him a sailing, right over the main,
He shall never come to England to plague you again."

Now when this young damsel she heard of the news,
Away to the captain she hastily goes,
Saying—" Captain, bold captain, I have bad news to tell,
You have got my young sailor for a transport to sell."

She out of her pocket pulled handfuls of gold,
And down on the deck the guineas they rolled;
Crying—"Captain, bold captain, all this I'll give you,
For my jolly young sailor, my right and my due."

" Oh no," says the Captain, "that never can be,
For only last night he was sold unto me;
I will send him a sailing right over the main,
He will never come to England to court you again."

" Bad luck to my father, wherever he be,
I feel in my own heart he has ruined me;
I'll away to my couch and then lay myself down,
And day and night long for my sailor I'll mourn."

THE BRITISH MAN OF WAR.

'Twas down in yonder meadows I carelessly did stray,
Where I beheld a lady fair with some young sailor gay;
Says he, " My lovely Susan, I soon must leave the shore
To cross the briny ocean in a British man o' war."

Then Susan fell to weeping: " Oh sailor," she did say,
" How can you be so venturesome, and throw yourself away?
For when that I am twenty-one I shall receive my store,—
Jolly sailor do not venture in a British man o' war."

"Oh Susan, lovely Susan, the truth to you I'll tell,
 The British flag's insulted, and England knows it well;
 I may be crowned with laurels, so like a jolly tar
 I'll face the walls of China in a British man o' war."

"Oh sailor do not venture to face the proud Chinese,
 For they will prove more treacherous than any Portuguese;
 And from some deadly dagger you may receive a scar,—
 So turn your inclination from a British man o' war."

"But Susan, lovely Susan, the time will quickly pass,
 So come down to the ferry house and take a parting glass;
 My shipmates they are waiting to row me from the shore,
 And I'll sail for England's glory in a British man o' war."

The sailor took his handkerchief and cut it fair in two,
Saying, "Susan keep one half for me, I'll do the same for you;
The bullets may surround me, and the cannons loudly roar,
But I'll fight for fame and Susan in a British man o' war."

A few more words together, her love let go her hand,
His shipmates launched their boat and rowed so merrily from land;
The sailor waved his handkerchief when far away from shore,
Pretty Susan blessed her sailor in a British man o' war.

Polly Oliver.

Chappell, in his Popular Music, mentions this song, and gives four lines of it as a specimen.

One night as Polly Oliver lay dozing in bed,
A comical fancy came into her head;
"No father nor mother shall make me false prove,
I'll enlist for a soldier and follow my love."
With coat, waistcoat, and breeches, and a sword by her side,
Her father's black gelding as a dragoon she did ride.

She rode till she came to fair London town,
Where she put up her horse at the the sign of the Crown;
When who should be there—in truth just come in,
But her true love, the captain, who tried her to win.
"Good even to you, my bold captain," she cried,
"I've a letter from Polly, your joy and your pride."

When he opened the letter, a guinea he found,
For he and his comrades to drink Polly's health round;
And supper being over, Polly hung down her head,
And called for a candle to light her to bed;
When up spoke the captain, "I've a bed at my ease,
And you may lie with me, countryman, if you please."

"To lie with a captain is a dangerous thing,
But I'm a new soldier come to fight for the king,
And we must obey orders by sea and by land,
And as you are my captain I'll obey your command."
So the captain and Polly together they lied,
And little thought he who it was by his side.

So early next morning Polly Oliver arose,
And dressed herself neat in her maidenly clothes;
And cried, when the captain came down from above,
"Look! here stands your Polly, your joy and your love."
"Now welcome, my Polly, I'll make you my wife,
And we'll live happy together all the days of our life."

THE RAMBLING SAILOR.

I am a sailor stout and bold,
   Long time I've ploughed the ocean;
I've fought for my King, and country too,
   For honour and promotion.
But now, brother sailors, I must bid you adieu,
No more to the seas will I go with you;
But I'll travel the country through and through,
And be a rambling sailor.

When I set foot in Portsmouth town,
   I met with lasses plenty;
I boldly steppéd up to one—
   Her age was five and twenty.
Said I, "My dear, be of good cheer,
Come, go with me, you need not fear,
We'll travel the country far and near,
And I'll be a rambling sailor."

Then I went up to Chatham town,
   And there were lasses bonny;
I boldly steppéd up to one
   To court her for her money.
Said I, "My dear, what do you choose?
Here's gin and rum, let's no time lose,
And here's a pair of new silk shoes,
To travel with a rambling sailor.

And if you wish to know my name,
   My name it is Tom Transom;
I have a commission from the King
   To court all the girls that are handsome.
With my false heart and flattering tongue,
I'll court them all, both old and young;
I'll court them all, but marry none,
And still be a rambling sailor."

THE MERMAID.

A somewhat different version of this song, with the tune, is in Chappell's Popular Music.

   'Twas a Friday morning when we set sail,
    And our ship was not far from land,
   When there we spied a fair pretty maid
    With a comb and a glass in her hand.
 Oh, the raging seas they did roar,
  And the stormy winds they did blow,
While we poor sailor boys were all up aloft,
 And the land lubbers lying down below, below, below,
 And the land lubbers lying down below.

   Then up spoke the captain of our gallant ship,
    And a mariner good was he—
   "I have married a wife in fair London town,
    And this night a widow she will be."
    Oh, the raging seas they did roar, &c.

   Then up spoke the cabin boy of our gallant ship,
    And a brave little boy was he—
   "I've a father and a mother in old Portsmouth town,
    And this night they will both weep for me."
    Oh, the raging seas they did roar, &c.

   Then up spoke a seaman of our gallant ship,
    And a well spoken man was he—
   "For want of a long boat we shall all be drowned,
    And shall sink to the bottom of the sea."
    Oh, the raging seas they did roar, &c.

   Then three times round went that gallant ship,
    And down like a stone sank she;
   The moon shone bright and the stars gave their light,
    But they were all at the bottom of the sea.
    Oh, the raging seas they did roar, &c.

THE LOSS OF THE RAMILIES.

In February, 1760, Admiral Boscawen, with six sail of the line, sailed from Plymouth to join the British fleet off Quiberon. A violent storm arising, the squadron, much damaged, put back to Plymouth, but the Ramilies, of 90 guns, with a crew of over 700 men, was driven ashore near Bolt Head, in Devonshire, and totally wrecked. The captain (Taylor) and the whole of the crew, with the exception of a midshipman and 25 men, perished in this fatal shipwreck —one of the most disastrous that ever happened in the Royal Navy.

You soldiers and sailors, draw near and attend
Unto these few lines that have lately been penned;
I'll tell you the dangers of the salt seas,
And the fatal destruction of the Ramilies.
    Oh, the fatal Ramilies.

Seven hundred and seventy brave men had we,
With ninety good guns to bear us company;
But as we were sailing, to our sad surprise,
A most terrible storm began for to rise.
    Oh, the fatal Ramilies.

The sea looked like fire, and rolled mountains high,
While our seamen did weep, and our captain did cry,
" Men, all mind your business, do all that you can;
For if this gale lasts, we are lost every man."
    Oh, the fatal Ramilies.

We all went to work, our lives for to save,
While our masts and our rigging did beat the salt wave;
" Bear away," cried our captain, " your skill do not spare,
So long as we've sea room, the less we've to fear."
    Oh, the fatal Ramilies.

In a few moments after, with a most dreadful shock,
The poor Ramilies she dashed on a rock;
'Twould have made any Jew's heart, or Turk's, to relent,
To hear the dismal cries when first down she went.
    Oh, the fatal Ramilies.

All you that are willing to do a good deed,
In relieving the widows in this time of need,
Bear a hand to assist them, and God will you bless
With happiness greater than I can express.
    Oh, the fatal Ramilies.

THE DEATH OF GENERAL WOLFE.

(Killed at Quebec, September 13th, 1760, in the moment of victory.) Probably the composition of a contemporary ballad singer.

Brave General Wolfe, to his men said he,
" Come, my brave lads, and follow me
To yonder mountains, that are so high,
All for the honour of your King and country."

The French were on the mountains high,
While we, poor lads, did in the valleys lie;
But we saw them falling like motes in the sun,
In the smoke and fire from our British guns.

The very first volley they gave to us,
Wounded our general in his left breast;
He sat down, saying, (for he could not stand)
" Fight on boldly, for while I live I'll give command.

Here is my treasure, it is all in gold;
Take it, and share it, for my blood runs cold;
Take it, and part it," General Wolfe did say,
" You lads of honour, who make such gallant play.

When to old England you do return,
Pray tell my parents I am dead and gone;
And tell my tender old mother dear,
Not to weep for a death I wished to share.

'Tis fourteen years since I first begun,
At honour's call—but my race is run.
Let all commanders do, as I before,—
Be a soldier's friend, and they'll fight for evermore."

PAUL JONES, THE PIRATE.

Paul Jones was the assumed name of John Paul, a noted naval adventurer of the last century, who was born near Kirkcudbright in 1747. He followed a seafaring life, and after some voyages to the West Indies and America, settled in Virginia in 1773. On the breaking out of the war between England and America, he entered the naval service of the United States, and being appointed to the Ranger, a privateer, he alarmed his native coast of Scotland and the adjoining coast of England; captured the Drake sloop of war, and anchored in Brest with his plunder and prisoners. In 1779, with the Bonhomme Richard, of 40 guns, the Alliance, 40 guns, the Pallas, 32 guns, and a twelve-gun brig, he sailed again for the northern coast of England; and on September 23rd, off Flamborough Head, performed the most notable exploit in his career, which is the subject of the following song. On that day he fell in with a British convoy from the Baltic, guarded by the Serapis, 44 guns, commanded by Captain Pearson; and the Countess of Scarborough, 22 guns, and fought one of the most desperate naval engagements on record. The greater part of the convoy escaped; but after a contest which lasted from about half-past seven till nearly midnight, both the British ships were compelled to strike to the enemy. Jones's own ship, the Richard, was so shattered, that she sank directly after the action; but the other vessels and their prizes got safely into the Texel, and the successful Commodore was shortly afterwards presented with a sword of honour by Louis XVI. of France. After the peace of 1783, Jones entered the Russian service, and as Rear-Admiral, commanded a squadron against the Turks. He died at Paris in

1792. Though popularly represented to be a Pirate, he certainly was none; but he was the first naval commander that compelled the English flag to strike to the ensign of America. In J. F. Cooper's novel, "The Pilot," he is one of the principal characters.

A spanking fine frigate, the Richard by name,
Mounting 44 guns, with the Pallas, there came
To cruise in the Channel, off old England's shore,
And Paul Jones was the name of our brave commodore.

We had not been a cruising but days two or three,
When the man at the mast-head a sail he did see;
It was the Serapis, a large forty-four,—
Her convoy stood on for the old Yorkshire shore.

At length the proud Briton came up alongside,
With a long speaking-trumpet, "Whence come you?" he cried,
" Come, answer me quickly—I have hailed you before—
Or else a broadside I will into you pour."

We received the broadside from the proud Englishmen,
But soon the brave Richard returned it agen;
'Twas broadside for broadside, five glasses we run,
When the undaunted flag of the Richard came down.

Our gunner was frightened; to Paul Jones he came,
Saying, "Our ship's making water, and is likewise in flame."
Our commodore thus to the gunner replied,
" If we can do no better, we will sink alongside."

Our powder and shot were both well nigh gone,
But the state of the British was worse than our own;
Their ports were beat in, and fearing to drown,
And their ship was on fire, so they hauled their flag down.

Well, now my brave lads, we have taken a prize,
A large forty-four, and a twenty likewise,
With twenty-five merchantmen, loaded with stores;
So we'll alter our course to the American shores.

THE LOWLANDS LOW.

One of the most curious old songs ever heard in the Island, and now almost forgotten. Judging from internal evidence, it would seem to belong to the time of Elizabeth, or James I.; the "Lowlands" probably being Holland, and the "Spanish Gallee" pointing to the struggle of the Low Countries with Spain for independence. A song having much general resemblance to this, but longer, and in a very different form, is printed in Mrs. Gordon's life of her father, Professor Wilson, with whom it was a favourite.

Our ship she was called the Golden Vanitee;
We had sailed from our port about miles fifty-three,
When up came with us a Spanish gallee,
    To sink us in the Lowlands low.

Our master wrung his hands, but our little cabin boy
Said, " What will you give me master, if I do them destroy ?"
"Oh, I will give you gold, and my daughter too, with joy,
    If you sink them in the Lowlands low."

The boy gave a nod, and then jumped into the sea,
And he swam till he came to the Spanish gallee;
He climbed up aboard, and below to work went he
    To sink them in the Lowlands low.

For this boy he had an auger that bored twenty holes in twice;
And while some were playing cards, and some were playing dice,
Through the bottom of the ship he bored it in a trice,
    And he sunk them in the Lowlands low.

The galley she went down, but the boy swam back again,
Crying, " Master, pick me up, or I shall soon be slain;
Pray heave to me a rope, or I shall sink in the main;
    For I've sunk them in the Lowlands low."

" I will not pick you up," the master loudly cried,
" I will not heave a rope," the master he replied,
" I will kill you, I will sink you, I will leave you in the tide ;
    I will sink you in the Lowlands low."

The boy he swam around the ship from side to side,
But he could not get aboard, so he sank, and he died ;
And they left him where he was to go down with the tide, —
    So they sunk him in the Lowlands low.

THE HONEST THRESHERMAN.

In the Roxburgh collection there is a long ballad, entitled " The Nobleman's Generous Kindness," of which this song seems to be an abridgment. The facts are identical, and the ballad loses little by compression.

There was an old thresherman,
    An old thresherman of late ;
He many had in family,
    And not too much to eat.
For he had seven children,
    And most of them were small ;
With nothing but his labour
    To maintain them all.

There was an old gentleman
  Who this thresher met one day,
And stepping up unto him,
  He unto him did say :
" How do you maintain your wife
  And your large family ?
For however you can manage
  Is a mystery to me."

" Why sir, sometimes I reap,
  And sometimes I do mow ;
And sometimes a hedging
  Or a ditching I do go ;
There's nothing comes amiss,
  I can thrash and I can plough ;
And so I get my living
  By the sweat of my brow.

My wife too, sir, is willing
  To help me with my yoke ;
We happy live together,
  Nor each other do provoke.
I carry home my wages,
  To do her best she strives ;
I truly think I have, sir,
  One of the best of wives."

" Well done, my honest thresher,
  You speak well of your wife ;
I'll provide for you a maintenance
  For the rest part of your life.
There are fifty of broad acres
  Of good land I'll give to thee,
For to maintain your wife
  And your large family."

Now this old thresherman,
  His day's work being done,
Home to his wife and family
  He speedily did run.
His children flocked around him
  With their prittling prattling noise,
And this is the greatest comfort
  That a poor man enjoys.

THE JOLLY WAGGONER.

When first I went a waggoning,
  A waggoning did go,
I filled my parents' hearts full
  Of sorrow, grief, and woe ;

And many are the hardships
  That I have since gone through;
    But sing woa, my lads—sing woa!
    Drive on my lads—I-o!
    There's none that lead such a merry life
    As the jolly waggoners do.

Now the night is cold and dark,
  And I'm wet through to the skin,
But I'll bear it with contentment
  Till I get to my inn;
And then I'll get a drinking
  With the landlord and his friends;
    But sing woa, my lads—sing woa! &c.

The summer it is coming—
  What pleasure we shall see;
The small birds are a singing
  On every bush and tree;
And the blackbirds and the thrushes
  Are a whistling in the groves;
    But sing woa, my lads—sing woa! &c.

Now Michaelmas is coming—
  What pleasures we shall find;
It will make the gold to fly, my boys,
  Like chaff before the wind;
And every lad shall take his lass
  And set her on his knee;
    So sing woa, my lads—sing woa!
    Drive on my lads—I-o!
    There's none that lead such a merry life
    As the jolly waggoners do.

THE FARMER'S BOY.

This song is well known in many parts of England. It is a popular bucolic ditty, and always formed part of the stock of the itinerant ballad singers.

The sun had set beyond yon hills,
  When across the dreary moor,
Weary and lame, a boy there came
  Up to a farmer's door.
" Can you tell me if any there be
  That will give me employ,
To plough and sow, and reap and mow,
  And be a farmer's boy?

My father is dead, and my mother's left
  With her five children small;
And what is worse for mother still,
  I'm the oldest of them all.
Though little, I am not afraid of work,
  If you'll give me employ,
To plough and sow, and reap and mow,
  And be a farmer's boy.

And if that you won't me employ,
  One favour I've to ask,
That you shelter me till break of day
  From this cold winter's blast;
And at break of day, I'll trudge away
  Elsewhere to seek employ,
To plough and sow, and reap and mow,
  And be a farmer's boy."

The Mistress said, "We'll try the lad,
  No further let him seek";
" O do, dear father," the daughter cried,
  With tears running down her cheeks,
" For those that will work, 'tis hard to want food,
  And to wander for employ;
Don't turn him away, but let him stay,
  And be a farmer's boy."

In time the lad became a man,
  And the good old farmer died;
He left the lad the farm he had,
  And the daughter for his bride.
The boy that was—now a farmer is,
  And he oft times thinks with joy,
Of the lucky day he came that way,
  To be a farmer's boy.

The Barley Mow Song.

This is a favourite Harvest Song, with an accumulative chorus; every verse repeating the whole of the measures named in the verses preceding. The song can be extended almost *ad libitum.*

We'll drink out of the nipperkin, boys,
Here's a good health to the barley-mow,
The nipperkin and the jolly brown bowl;
So merrily we will sing, my boys,
Here's a good health to the barley-mow.

We'll drink out of the quarter-pint, boys,
Here's a good health to the barley-mow;
The quarter-pint, nipperkin, and the jolly brown bowl, &c.

We'll drink out of the half-pint, boys,
Here's a good health to the barley-mow;
The half-pint, quarter-pint, nipperkin, &c.

We'll drink out of the pint, my boys,
Here's a good health to the barley-mow;
The pint, half-pint, &c.

We'll drink out of the quart, my boys,
Here's a good health to the barley-mow;
The quart, pint, half-pint, &c.

We'll drink out of the half-gallon, boys,
Here's a good health to the barley-mow;
The half-gallon, quart, pint, &c.

We'll drink out of the gallon, my boys,
Here's a good health to the barley-mow;
The gallon, half-gallon, quart, &c.

We'll drink out of the peck, my boys,
Here's a good health to the barley-mow;
The peck, gallon, half-gallon, &c.

We'll drink out of the half-bushel, boys,
Here's a good health to the barley-mow;
The half-bushel, bushel, peck, &c,

We'll drink out of the bushel, my boys,
Here's a good health to the barley-mow;
The bushel, half-bushel, peck, &c.

We'll drink out of the kilderkin, boys,
Here's a good health to the barley-mow;
The kilderkin, bushel, half-bushel, &c.

We'll drink out of the hogshead, my boys,
Here's a good health to the barley-mow;
The hogshead, kilderkin, bushel, half-bushel, peck, gallon,
    half-gallon, quart, pint, half-pint, quarter-pint, nipperkin,
    and the jolly brown bowl;
So merrily we will sing, my boys,
Here's a good health to the barley-mow.

The song was often extended to the pipe, butt, tun, pond, well, river, &c., till the sea was reached, all of which was recapitulated at the end of the last verse.

The Song of Sixpence.

I had a sixpence, oh my jolly sixpence,
  I loved my sixpence as much as I loved my life;
A penny I will spend, and another I will lend,
  And fourpence carry home to my wife.

I had a fourpence, oh my jolly fourpence,
  I loved my fourpence as much as I loved my life;
A penny I will spend, and another I will lend,
  And twopence carry home to my wife.

I had a twopence, oh my jolly twopence,
  I loved my twopence as much as I loved my life;
A penny I will spend, and another I will lend,
  And nothing carry home to my wife.

Now I have nothing, oh my jolly nothing,
  I love nothing so much as I love my life;
So nothing I can spend, and nothing I can lend,
  And I'll take nothing home to my wife.

My Boy Billy.

Where have *you* been all the day,
    My boy Billy?
Where have *you* been all the day,
    Pretty Billy, tell me?
I have been all the day
Courting of a lady gay,
But she's a young thing
    Just come from her mammy O.

Is she fit to be thy love,
    My boy Billy?
Is she fit to be thy love,
    Pretty Billy, tell me?
She's as fit to be my love
As my hand is for my glove,
But she's a young thing
    Just come from her mammy O.

What work can she do,
    My boy Billy?
Can she bake and can she brew,
    Pretty Billy, tell me?
She can brew and she can bake,
And she can make a good lard cake,
But she's a young thing
    Just come from her mammy O.

Can she scrub and clean the house,
    My boy, Billy?
Can she scrub and clean the house,
    Pretty Billy tell me?
She can scrub and clean the house,
As quick as a cat can catch a mouse;
Although she's but a young thing
    Just come from her mammy O.

How old may she be,
    My boy Billy?
How old may she be,
    Pretty Billy tell me?
Twice six, twice seven,
Twice twenty and eleven;
But oh, she's but a young thing
    Just come from her mammy O.

WHAT IS YOUR ONE O?

The following curious song is certainly the most ancient in origin of any found in the Island; being really a Christianized version of a rhythmic chant derived from the ceremonies of the Druids. In the north-western parts of France a Latin version is current, and sung by the children of the peasantry. It runs thus—

> "Dic mihi quid unus?
> Unus est Deus,
> Qui regnat in cœlis.
>
> Dic mihi quid duo?
> Duo testamenta,
> Unus est Deus, &c.
>
> Dic mihi qui sunt tres?
> Tres sunt patriarchæ,
> Duo sunt testamenta,
> Unus est Deus
> Qui regnat in cœlis."

And so on to the number twelve. Four are the Evangelists; five, the books of Moses; six, the pitchers at the marriage in Cana; seven, the sacraments; eight, the beatitudes; nine, the chorus of angels; ten, the commandments; eleven, the stars as seen by Joseph; twelve, the Apostles. The original Druidic rhythm combined precepts on Cosmogony, Astrology, and Theology, with Medicine and History; and the references in the Christianized version to the lily white boys clothed all in green, the seven stars, and the triple Trine, unmistakably proclaim its derivation. Versions of the song are to be met with in various parts of England, but all when complete go to the number twelve, and all more or less agree in phraseology. In singing, at the end of each verse all the terms occurring in those preceding are recapitulated.

> What is your one O?
> When the one is left alone,
> No more he can be seen O.

What is your two O?
Two and two—the lily white boys
Clothed all in green O,
When the one is left alone,
No more he can be seen O.

What is your three O?
Three, three—the Kings O,
Two and two—the lily white boys
Clothed all in green O, &c.

What is your four O?
Four—the four Evangelists,
Three, three—the Kings O,
Two and two—the lily white boys, &c.

What is your five O?
Five is odd and even O,
Four—the four Evangelists,
Three, three—the Kings O, &c.

What is your six O?
Six, six—the weaver,
Five is odd and even O,
Four—the four Evangelists, &c.

What is your seven O?
Seven stars in the sky,
Six, six—the weaver,
Five is odd and even O, &c.

What is your eight O?
Eight—the eight Archangels,
Seven stars in the sky,
Six, six—the weaver, &c.

What is your nine O?
Nine, nine—the triple Trine,
Eight—the eight Archangels,
Seven stars in the sky, &c.

What is your ten O?
Ten—the Ten Commandments,
Nine, nine—the triple Trine,
Eight—the eight Archangels, &c.

What is your eleven O?
Eleven—the Gospel preachers,
Ten—the Ten Commandments,
Nine, nine—the triple Trine, &c.

What is your twelve O?
Twelve—the twelve Apostles,
Eleven—the Gospel preachers,
Ten—the Ten Commandments,
Nine, nine—the triple Trine,

Eight—the eight Archangels,
Seven stars in the sky,
Six, six—the weaver,
Five is odd and even O,
Four—the four Evangelists,
Three, three—the Kings O,
Two and two—the lily white boys,
Clothéd all in green O,
When the one is left alone,
No more he can be seen O.

The copies of this song, oral and written, collected by the Editor, were so exceedingly corrupt as to make it a matter of considerable difficulty to get at the original form of the verses. For example—verse 8: one copy gave it as "Eight—the *Gaberandrist;*" and another, "Eight—the *Cablerangers;*" and only after some research was the real reading discovered. In several of the verses, however, all the copies agreed.

николаs wood.

This song is of some antiquity, probably dating from the time of Charles I., or earlier. In 1630, a tract or chap book in 4to was published by John Taylor, the Water Poet, entitled, "The great Eater of Kent, part of the Admirable Teeth and Stomach Exploits of Nicholas Wood;" which says: "This noble Nicholas hath made an end of a hog all at once, as if it had been but a rabbit sucker, and presently after, for fruit to recreate his palate, he swallowed three pecks of damsons. Two loins of mutton, and one loin of veal, were but as three sprats to him. Once at Sir Warham St. Leger's house, he showed himself so valiant of teeth and stomach that he ate as much as would have served and sufficed thirty men, so that his belly was like to turn bankrupt and break, but that the serving men turned him to the fire, and anointed his paunch with grease and butter to make it stretch and hold; and afterwards being laid in bed, he slept eight hours and fasted all the while; which when the knight understood, he commanded him to be laid in the stocks, and there to endure as long a time as he had lain bedrid with eating." At Lord Wotton's he devoured 84 rabbits at one sitting, and once swallowed 18 yards of black puddings for his breakfast. Fuller, in his "Worthies," notices the diseased appetite of Nicholas Wood, of Halingbourne, in Kent. He was a man of some means, but spent all in providing for his belly, and died in poverty. The song certainly refers to the same person, and was taken down from the recollections of an old lady nearly 80 years old.

"Oh, when shall we be married,
　My sweet dear Nicholas Wood?"
"Well, we'll be married on Monday,
　For I think it quite proper we should."

"What, shan't we be married before,
　My sweet dear Nicholas Wood?"
"What, would you be married on Sunday?
　I think the young girl's gone mad."

"What shall we have for our dinner,
　My own sweet Nicholas Wood?"
"Oh, we'll have beans and bacon,
　For I think it is wondrous good."
"What, shan't we have nothing besides,
　My sweet dear Nicholas Wood?"
"What, would you have cocks and capons?
　Why sure the young girl's gone mad."

"Whom shall we have to our wedding,
　My sweet dear Nicholas Wood?"
"Oh, we'll have father and mother,
　For I think it is proper we should."
"What, shan't we have nobody else,
　My sweet dear Nicholas Wood?"
"What, would you have lords and ladies?
　I think the young girl's gone mad."

"What shall we have for supper,
　My sweet dear Nicholas Wood?"
"Oh, I'll have beans and bacon,
　There's nothing that's half so good."
"You swallowed all that for your dinner,
　My sweet dear Nicholas Wood."
"Then give me a peck of pottage,
　Or hunger will drive me mad."

While Joan's Ale was New.

Versions of this well-known song, with the tune, are to be found in D'Urfey's "Pills to Purge Melancholy," and in Chappell's "Popular Music." The song as sung in the Isle of Wight differs in many places from both of these copies, and has one stanza not found in either of them. The title, at least, of this song is as old as the sixteenth century. On October the 26th, 1594, "A Ballett entitled Jone's Ale is Newe," was entered in the books of the Stationers' Company; and the burden of the song called the Jovial Tinker, mentioned in Ben Jonson's "Tale of a Tub," is "Joan's Ale is New."

　　　There were some jovial fellows,
　　　Went over the hills together,
　　　In spite of wind and weather,
　　　　To join a jovial crew.

They called for bottles of ale and sherry,
And sat themselves down for to be merry;
"You're welcome as flowers in May," said Jerry,
    While Joan's ale was new, my boys,
    While Joan's ale was new.

The first that came in was a tinker,
And he was no small beer drinker;
From strong ale he was no shrinker,
    To join the jovial crew.
He sat himself down at once in the settle,
And called for a pot of the very best fettle,
And swore he'd go and mend a kettle,
    While Joan's ale was new, my boys,
    While Joan's ale was new.

The next that came in was a soldier,
With his firelock on his shoulder,
And no one looked more bolder,
    Among the jovial crew.
He threw his firelock on the ground,
And said, now he'd good liquor found,
He boldly drank their healths all round,
    While Joan's ale was new, my boys,
    While Joan's ale was new.

The next that came in was a mason;
His hammer it wanted facing,
And he boldly entered the place in,
    To join the jovial crew.
He threw his hammer against the wall,
And wished the churches and chapels might fall,
For then would be work for masons all,
    While Joan's ale was new, my boys,
    While Joan's ale was new.

The next that came in was a dyer;
He sat himself down by the fire,
For it was his heart's desire
    To join the jovial crew.
He told the landlord to his face,
The chimney corner was his place;
And there he sat and drank apace,
    While Joan's ale was new, my boys,
    While Joan's ale was new.

The next that came in was a hatter,
To see what was the matter;
And he began to chatter
    Among the jovial crew.
He threw his hat upon the ground,
And swore every man should spend his crown,

And loudly called for pots all round,
    While Joan's ale was new, my boys,
    While Joan's ale was new.

The last that came in was a ragman,
With his ragbag over his shoulder;
And nobody could be bolder,
    Among the jovial crew.
The landlord's daughter she came in,
He kissed her over the mouth and chin,
And asked her to take a glass of gin,
    While Joan's ale was new, my boys,
    While Joan's ale was new.

JOLLY FELLOWS.

The music of this song is in Chappell's "Popular Music," but is different and inferior to the tune sung in the Island. The song itself is evidently founded on some verses in Fletcher's play of "The Bloody Brother, or Rollo Duke of Normandy," Act I., scene 2.

" Drink to day and drown all sorrow,
You shall perhaps not do it to-morrow;
But while you have it, use your breath,—
There is no drinking after death.

Wine works the heart up, wakes the wit;
There is no cure 'gainst age but it;
It helps the headache, cough, and tissic,
And is for all diseases physic.

Then let us swill, boys, for our health;
Who drinks well—loves the commonwealth;
And he that will to bed go sober,
Falls with the leaf still in October."

[In singing, the third line of each verse is thrice repeated.]

Come landlord, fill the flowing bowl,
    Until it does run over;
For to night we'll merry be,
For to night we'll merry be,
For to night we'll merry be,
    And to morrow we'll get sober.

He that drinks strong beer,
    And goes to bed mellow,
Lives as he ought to live,
    And dies a hearty fellow.

> But he that drinks small beer,
>   And goes to bed sober,
> Falls as the leaves fall,
>   That fall in chill October.
>
> Strong beer cures the gout,
>   The colic, and the phthisic;
> And it is for all men
>   The very best of physic.
>
> He that courts a pretty girl,
>   He courts her for his pleasure;
> Fool if he ever marries her,
>   Without great store of treasure.
>
> So now come let us dance and sing,
>   And drive away all sorrow;
> For perhaps we may not
>   Meet again to morrow.

DICK TURPIN, OR TURPIN HERO.

It is singular to find the fame of Turpin, one of the most cowardly and desperate ruffians that ever lived, so far removed from the scene of his exploits. His depredations were chiefly confined to Essex and the adjoining counties; and after committing countless robberies, and at least one murder, he was hanged at York in April, 1739. In a pedlar's collection of songs published in the latter part of the last century, is a long rambling ballad, entitled "Turpin's Valiant Exploits; to be sung to its own proper tune;" the first part of which is a very similar version of the circumstance related in the song as sung in the Isle of Wight. It is probably almost contemporary with the facts it relates.

> " On Houndslow Heath as I rode o'er,
>   I spied a lawyer riding before;
> ' Kind sir,' said I, ' are you not afraid
>   Of Turpin, that mischievous blade?'
>   O rare Turpin hero, O rare Turpin O."

Turpin proceeds to say that his money is safely hidden in the heel of his boot; and the lawyer, with a confidence rare in one of his profession, acquaints his companion that *his* gold is stowed away in his cape, which of course is presently taken off by the highwayman.

> " This caused the lawyer sore to fret,
>   To think he was so fairly bit;
> For soon was he robbed of all his store,
>   Because he knew how to lye for more.
>   O rare Turpin, &c."

After fifteen more verses describing "Turpin's valour," the ballad concludes with—

"Now Turpin he's condemned to die,
To hang upon yon gallows high;
Whose legacy is a strong rope,
For shooting of a dunghill cock.
  O rare Turpin, &c."

A very similar version, with the tune, which is different from that sung in the Island, is in Chappel's "Popular Music."

As Turpin was riding across the moor,
He saw a lawyer on before;
He rode up to him, and thus did say,
"Have you seen Dick Turpin ride this way?"
  To my hero, Turpin hero,
  I am the valiant Turpin O.

"I've not seen Turpin ride this way,
Nor do I wish to see him to day;
For I'm just come out of the courts of law,
And I have my money here under my paw."
  To my hero, &c.

"Oh then," says Turpin, "I've been cute,
I've hid my money in my boot";
"Ah ha," said the lawyer, "he shan't find mine,
For I sewed it up in my cape behind."
  To my hero, &c.

So they rode till they came to Woodbury hill,
When he bade the lawyer to stand still;
"The cape of your coat, it must come off,
For my horse is in want of a saddle cloth."
  To my hero, &c.

"So now you are robbed of all your store,
You may go to law and seek for more;
And if my name in request you bring,
My name it is called Dick Turpin."
  To my hero, &c.

"I am the last of Turpin's gang,
My sentence is—I'm to be hanged;
Two thousand pounds I have got by me,
I'll give Jack Ketch for a legacy."
  To my hero, &c.

The Jolly Butchers.

From its subject and phraseology, this song appears to belong to the northern parts of England. Its date is uncertain.

It is of two jolly butchers,
    As I have heard them say,
They took five hundred guineas,
    All on one market day.
They were riding home together,
    As fast as they could ride,
When Johnson said to Wilson,
    " I hear some woman's cries.

I'll stop, I'll stop," said Johnson,
    " I'll stop and search," said he;
"Oh no, oh no," said Wilson,
    " For robbéd we might be."
But Johnson, being a gallant man,
    Did search the groves all round,
And found a wretched woman
    With her hair pinned to the ground.

" How came you here, my lassie,
    How came you here stark bound,
How came you here stark naked,
    With your hair pinned to the ground?"
" They robbéd me, they strippéd me,
    My hands and feet they bound,
And left me here stark naked,
    With my hair pinned to the ground."

So Johnson, being a gallant man,
    And of a gallant mind,
Did take his coat from off his back,
    And set her up behind.
But then, up stepped three stalwart men
    With swords and staves in hand,
And Johnson stabbéd two of them,
    As soon as they bade him stand.

He then fought with the other one,
    The woman he did not mind;
But she slyly crept up to him,
    And stabbéd him behind.
She shall be hanged in chains of gold
    For the murder she has done;
She has killed the finest butcher
    That ever the sun shone on.

THE CARRION CROW.

Captain Grose, in his " Olio," quotes this song, and writes on it a burlesque commentary. It is always a favourite, and is at least as old as the time of Charles I. As sung in the Island, the

Carrion Crow cries "Pork, pork," instead of "Caa, caa," or "Croak, croak," given in other versions.

>The old carrion crow he sat upon an oak,
>   Fol the rol the diddle lol the dido;
>Watching a tailor a cutting out a cloak,
>   Heigh ho, the old carrion crow
>   Cries, Pork, pork, fol the rol the diddle lol the dido.

>"Wife, go and fetch me my arrow and my bow,
>   Fol the rol the diddle lol the dido;
>That I may shoot this cursed carrion crow."
>   Heigh ho, the old carrion crow
>   Cries, Pork, pork, fol the rol the diddle lol the dido.

>The tailor he shot, but he missed his mark,
>   Fol the rol the diddle lol the dido,
>And shot his old sow right through and through her heart.
>   Heigh ho, the old carrion crow
>   Cries, Pork, pork, fol the rol the diddle lol the dido.

>"Wife, go and bring me some treacle in a spoon,
>   Fol the rol the diddle lol the dido,
>Or our old sow she'll die very soon."
>   Heigh ho, the old carrion crow
>   Cries, Pork, pork, fol the rol the diddle lol the dido.

>The old sow she ran back against the wall,
>   Fol the rol the diddle lol the dido,
>And she swallowed the treacle, the wooden spoon and all.
>   Heigh ho, the old carrion crow
>   Cries, Pork, pork, fol the rol the diddle lol the dido.

>"Well, dang it," says the tailor, "I don't care a louse,
>   Fol the rol the diddle lol the dido,
>For I shall have black puddings, chitterlings and souse."
>   Heigh ho, the old carrion crow
>   Cries, Pork, pork, fol the rol the diddle lol the dido.

>And the bells they did ring, and the bells they did toll,
>   Fol the rol the diddle lol the dido,
>And the little pigs squeaked for the old sow's soul.
>   Heigh ho, the old carrion crow,
>   Cries, Pork, pork, fol the rol the diddle lol the dido.

The Fox.

A version of this song, but different, is printed in "Notes and Queries," 1854, as "An old Cornish Song."

> The fox jumped up one cold winter's night,
> The stars they were shining and the moon shone bright,
> "Oh ho," said the fox, "'tis a very fine night
> For me to go through the town O, town O,
> For me to go through the town O."
>
> So he went till he came to yonder stile,
> When he pricked up his ears and listened awhile;
> "Oh ho," said the fox, "'tis a very short mile
> From here to yonder town O, town O," &c.
>
> The fox when he came to the farmer's gate,
> Whom should he see but the farmer's drake:
> "I love you well for your master's sake,
> And long to be picking your bones O, bones O," &c.
>
> He caught the grey goose fast by the neck,
> And threw her up across his back,
> Which made the poor goose cry, quack, quack,
> And blood came trickling down O, down O, &c.
>
> Old Mother Slipperslopper jumped out of bed,
> And opened the window and popped out her head,
> "Oh, husband, oh, husband, the grey goose is dead,
> And the fox is gone through the town O, town O," &c.
>
> So the old man he ran to the top of the hill,
> And sounded his horn both loudly and shrill.
> "Blow away," said the fox, "as long as you will,
> But I have been through the town O, town O," &c.
>
> The fox he soon got back to his den,
> Where he had young cubs about nine or ten:
> "Oh welcome, daddy fox, we hope you'll go again,
> If you bring us such good meat from the town O, town O," &c.
>
> Said old daddy fox to his cubs and his wife,
> "This is the best goose I ever ate in all my life."
> So they tore up the goose without a fork or a knife,
> And the young cubs picked the bones O, bones O,
> And the young cubs picked the bones O.

Moss the Miller, and his Mare.

Moss was a miller, and one day to market went,
He sold his flour and bought a mare, for such was his intent;

Her back stuck up, her tail hung down, her ribs were almost
    bare,
" She only wants some corn," said Moss, as he brought home his
    mare.

Now Moss he was a little man, and a little mare did buy,
But for kicking and for biting there was none could her come
    nigh;
She could trot and she could canter, she would gallop here and
    there,
But one night no one could find her,—so Moss lost his mare.

Moss got up the next morning while all were fast asleep,
And round among the fields and lanes he carefully did creep;
Dead in a ditch he found her, but however she came there,
He knew no more than I do,—but Moss found his mare.

" Come rise, get up, you stupid mare," he unto her did say.
" Arise you beast, you drowsy beast, get up and come away,
For I must ride you to the town, so don't lie sleeping there ";
He put the halter on her head,—so Moss caught his mare.

THE CROCKERY WARE.

In London town once dwelt a spark,
Who courted a girl both gay and smart;
One night her company he did crave,
And at the last she gave him leave.
    Whack fol lol the diddle lol the day,
    Fol lol the ri de o.

Miss Kitty began for to contrive
How she her sweetheart might deceive;
In the middle of the room she placed a chair,
And loaded it with crockery ware.
    Whack fol lol the diddle lol the day, &c.

This young man rose in the middle of the night,
Thinking to go to his heart's delight,
But he missed his way, I do declare,
And fell right over the crockery ware.
    Whack fol lol, &c.

Her mother arose in a terrible fright,
And called out loudly for a light;
Said she, " Young man, how came you here,
A breaking of my crockery ware?"
    Whack fol lol, &c.

" Old girl," said he, " don't be surprised,
For I had great reason for to rise;

But I missed my way I do declare,
And I've broke my shins with your crockery ware.
  Whack fol lol, &c.

Miss Kitty lay laughing at the fun,
And seeing how the joke was carried on,
" If you missed your way, I do declare,
You must pay my mother for the crockery ware."
  Whack fol lol, &c.

Now all you gay young rambling sparks,
That love to ramble in the dark,
If you miss your way, I do declare,
You'll have to pay for the crockery ware.
  Whack fol lol, &c.

The Breeches.

Will's wife used often to declare,
She would herself the breeches wear,
And if her husband should resist,
For them she'd fight with nails and fist,
  To gain, to gain the breeches.

One day when they were at it driving,
Who should be master they were striving,
A bouncing rap came at the door,
Which made them for the time give o'er
  Fighting for the breeches.

Will ope'd the door, put out his head,
When thus to him the knocker said:
" The master of this house I want."
" See him just now," says Will, " you can't,
  Until he gets the breeches.

He and his wife can't well agree
As yet, who master is to be;
But in five minutes more or so,
Who master is, you then shall know,
  And who's to wear the breeches."

Will and his wife again engaged,
And a most furious contest waged;
Until poor Will was forced to yield,
And soundly drubbed, to quit the field;
  He lost, he lost the breeches."

His wife then went unto the door,
Just as poor Will had done before;
" Good morning friend—your business pray?
I'm master here,—I've gained the day,
  I wear, I wear the breeches."

WEARING THE BREECHES.

A song on a similar subject to the preceding, but inferior to it in humour.

Come all young men—I pray you draw near,
   And listen to my sad lamentation;
I courted a girl,—I loved her so dear,
   I loved her beyond admiration.
At length I made her my own wife,
   Not for her beauty, but for her riches;
But oftentimes it caused us strife,
   To know which one should wear the breeches.
        Whack, fal lal, &c.

If I e'er chanced to spend an hour
   Among my friends, and take my flagon,
My wife would come in to show her power,
   And battle about my ears like a dragon.
" Get out—begone—you drunken sot,
   Is this the way you spend my riches?
I'd better have kept what I had got,
   If I leave you to wear the breeches."
        Whack fal lal, &c.

She "dwarf" and "pigmy" did me call,
   My height being only four feet eleven;
My wife was looked upon as tall,
   Her height being nearly five feet seven.
The hedges I would sometimes strip,
   And leave them bare of rods and switches,
With which I'd threaten her to whip,—
   But still she swore she'd wear the breeches.
        Whack fal lal, &c.

One morning, with my tea and eggs,
   I sat contented by the fire;
She threw the teapot at my legs,
   Which quickly caused me to retire.
Thus wretched, I must sit and groan,
   Or else go limping on my crutches;
I wish I'd broke my collar bone,
   Before I'd let her wear the breeches.
        Whack fal lal, &c.

My wife fell sick—was very bad,
   And in a few weeks after died;
And I pretended to be sad,
   But the deuce of a tear for her I cried.

So let them all say what they will,
    She'll break no more of my plates and dishes;
For now she's dead, and her tongue lies still,
    Thank God she's got her *timbern breeches*.
        Whack fal lal, &c.

THE BONNY BUNCH OF ROSES O.

This song was probably written about fifty years ago, after the death of "young Napoleon," Duke of Reichstadt, who died at Schönbrunn, in 1832.

I walked abroad one morning,
    In the flowery month of June,
When the warbling feathered songsters
    Their notes so sweet did tune.
Then I espied a female,
    Who seemed in grief and woe,
Conversing with young Bonaparte,
    Concerning the bonny bunch of roses O.

"Oh," then said young Napoleon,
    And grasped his mother by the hand;
"Oh mother, pray have patience,
    Till I am able to command,
I'll raise a mighty army,
    And through terrible dangers go,
And in spite of all the universe,
    I'll gain the bonny bunch of roses O.

When first you saw great Bonaparte,
    You fell on your bended knee,
And asked your father's life of him,
    Which he granted graciously,
'Twas then he took his army,
    And o'er frozen realms did go,
Saying, 'First I'll conquer Moscow,
    Then gain the bonny bunch of roses O.'

He had men three hundred thousand,
    And likewise kings to join his throng;
He was so well provided,
    He'd enough to sweep the world along.
But when he came to Moscow,
    Overpowered by the driving snow;
All Moscow was a blazing,
    So he lost the bonny bunch of roses O."

" Now son, don't speak so venturesome,
   England is the heart of oak;
England, Ireland, and Scotland,
   Their unity has ne'er been broke.
And son—look at your father,
   In St. Helena he lies low,
And you will follow after
   If you strive for the bonny bunch of roses O."

" Oh mother, now adieu for ever,
   I know I'm on my dying bed;
If I had lived I should have been clever,
   But now I droop my youthful head.
But while our bones are mouldering,
   And weeping willows o'er us grow,
They will sing of bold Napoleon,
   How he lost the bonny bunch of roses O."

www.ingramcontent.com/pod-product-compliance
Lightning Source LLC
Chambersburg PA
CBHW020250170426
43202CB00008B/305